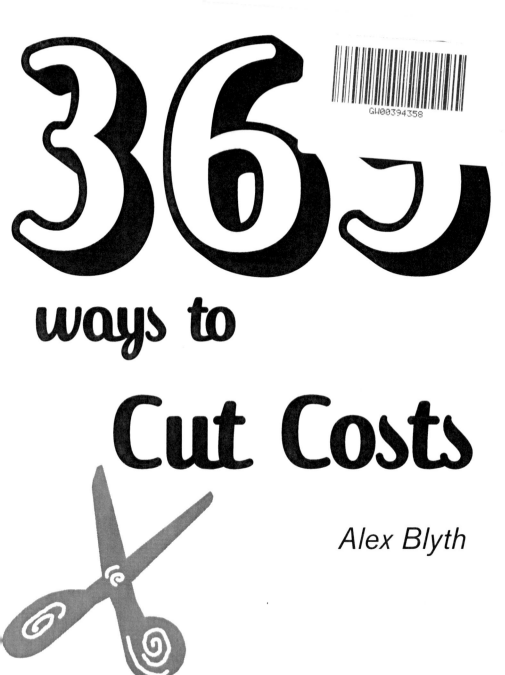

365

ways to

Cut Costs

Alex Blyth

DIRECTORY OF SOCIAL CHANGE

Published by
Directory of Social Change
24 Stephenson Way
London NW1 2DP
Tel. 08450 77 77 07; Fax 020 7391 4804
email publications@dsc.org.uk
www.dsc.org.uk
from whom further copies and a full books catalogue are available.

Directory of Social Change Northern Office
Federation House, Hope Street, Liverpool L1 9BW
Policy & Research 0151 708 0136

Directory of Social Change is a Registered Charity no. 800517

First published 2009

ISBN 978 1 906294 36 6

British Library Cataloguing in Publication Data
A catalogue record for this book is available from the British Library

Cover and text designed by Kate Bass
Typeset by Marlinzo Services, Frome
Printed and bound by CPI Antony Rowe, Chippenham

FSC
Mixed Sources
Product group from well-managed
forests and other controlled sources
Cert no. SGS-COC-2953
www.fsc.org
© 1996 Forest Stewardship Council

Contents

Foreword

The environment for charities has never been more exposed and demanding. The generosity of the public is under pressure, companies are less expansive in their corporate social responsibility plans, and the opportunities for charities to manage enterprises successfully to raise unrestricted income are reduced by the state of the economy.

Meanwhile, it is important that the voluntary sector flourishes to fill the gaps left behind as the state withdraws from the funding and provision of vital social services.

This compendium, published by the Directory of Social Change and compiled with insight by Alex Blyth, provides a helpful and timely guide for trustees and executives to make sensible, sustainable plans for efficiency. I commend it as essential reading for these times.

Michael Lake CBE

Michael Lake was Director General of Help the Aged for 12 years before guiding the charity to merger with Age Concern. He chairs the UK Age Research Forum and the British Gas Energy Trust, and is a trustee of the International Longevity Centre and of the Charities Aid Foundation.

About the author

Born in 1974, and with a degree in politics and philosophy from the University of York, Alex Blyth is a freelance journalist who has spent the past decade writing extensively about the voluntary sector.

He has written for publications such as *Third Sector, Professional Fundraising, Membership Today* and *Ethical Performance* on a wide range of topics, from the issues around street fundraising to whether charities should offer free plastic bags, from building effective websites to how to get the most from corporate partnerships.

He also writes widely for the business press, runs regular writing workshops, helps organisations to write their promotional material, and is called upon frequently to speak at industry events.

Alex lives with his wife Claire, and when he is not working, he usually can be found either trying to remember how to play cricket, or running around the green spaces of south-west London.

Introduction

Cost-cutting is always important to charities, but never more so than now. Research in October 2008 by the Charity Commission revealed that 38 per cent of charities had been affected by the economic downturn. This has brought the perennial issue of cost-cutting right to the top of the agenda.

Charities are always trying to keep their bills to a minimum, but the same research revealed that in the last few years more than half (54 per cent) had suffered with rising costs including energy, food and travel costs. Meanwhile, 40 per cent had experienced a drop in donations. This was all happening at the same time as demand for their services was increasing – 21 per cent said that demand for their services had risen in the past 12 months.

By December 2008, the payment processing firm Rapidata's *Charity Direct Debit Tracking Report 2009* was reporting that, after four years of falling cancellations in direct debits to charities, people were now beginning to cancel them. The NSPCC, which gets one-third of its income from regular giving, reported an increase in cancellation rates for payments through direct debits of about 14 per cent in 2008.

As we entered 2009 and the economic slowdown became a full-blown recession, the news worsened. A survey by Justgiving revealed that one-third of donors were considering cutting back their donations to charity. A Charities Aid Foundation poll showed that 41 per cent of charities were operating on less income than they had budgeted for, and more than half of charities affected by the recession had dipped into their reserves.

The Government announced its Third Sector Action Plan, and no one in the sector turned their noses up at the pledge of £42.5 million, but we all knew that it would take much more than that to protect charities of all shapes and sizes from cutbacks to services, from staff redundancies, and possibly even from liquidation.

The last two years have been tough indeed.

They have presented those running charities with unprecedented challenges. While we all know that charities are not businesses, charity managers have had to adopt a businesslike approach to their operations more than ever before. They have had to act to stem the tide of direct debit cancellations, to shore up their corporate donor base in any way that they can and to find ingenious new ways to acquire fresh donors. They have had to make difficult decisions on staffing levels and find increasingly innovative ways to cut costs.

In many ways, cutting those costs has been the most difficult aspect. As every successful businessperson knows, in tough times the last places you look to cut costs are sales, marketing and people development. Cutting back in those areas is a sure-fire way to squeeze the life out of any business.

The same is true of voluntary organisations. You can slash your fundraising budget and improve the balance sheet in the short term, but before long your income will fall and you will be in even worse trouble. You can reduce your headcount and freeze training, but before too long you will be trying to cope with a diminished and demoralised workforce. It is simply not an option.

So, what choices are left to you? Where can you make these cutbacks that are so essential to your organisation's survival?

This book contains 365 ideas for cutting costs without strangling your income or decimating your human resource. It covers a wide range of subjects, from salaries to tax, and from the Internet to public relations. Some are big ideas involving long-term projects such as merging with another charity, while others you can implement today, such as using online conferencing instead of travelling to meetings. You will be doing many of them already. Others you will know about, but might not have got around to putting into practice, and some will be new to you.

Don't try to implement all 365 ideas – you will simply end up running too many unfinished initiatives. Indeed not all of these 365 ideas will be relevant to your organisation. Instead, pick out a dozen: one for every month of the year ahead. Make a plan for putting them into practice and then do it, involving all those around you, and celebrating your achievements as you progress.

By doing this, you can genuinely transform your organisation. You will save your charity thousands of pounds and leave it well placed to survive the recession, but more than that: you will be turning a difficult situation into an opportunity. At the end of those 12 months your charity will have become an organisation which knows how to cut costs. It will be leaner, more creative, more dynamic – and better placed to deliver on its mission when the good times do return eventually.

Cutting costs is never easy, but armed with your determination to do it, and with the great ideas contained in these pages, you can make it happen.

So, let's get to work!

Chapter 1

Strategy

1. Prioritise cost-cutting at board level

Before you do anything else, you need your board of trustees to buy into the importance of cutting costs. No matter how obvious it seems to you that you have to cut costs, you must ensure that those at the top of your charity understand this. They have to set an example to the rest of the organisation to emphasise the importance of cost-cutting, and crucially, to approve difficult decisions that you will have to make. In simple terms, without their support you will never succeed.

So, schedule time with your trustees individually and as a group. Explain clearly why you need to cut costs. Show what will happen to your organisation if you fail to do so. Make them as enthusiastic about your project as you are.

2. Develop commercial skills on your board

As head of charities at accountancy firm Scott-Moncrieff and chair of the charities committee at the Institute of Chartered Accountants of Scotland, Gillian Donald has spent many years advising charities in Scotland on how they can cut their costs.

She offers this advice:

Get the right skills on your board of trustees and you will avoid many unnecessary costs. Begin with a skills audit – work out what skills you need to run your charity well, and see where the skill gaps on your board are. Then ensure you fill them.

Get the right skills on your board of trustees and you will avoid many unnecessary costs.

1

It's important to get a balance. You need to have the right professional skills for your charity. So, if you are a mental health charity you need to have psychiatrists. But you also need to have trustees with commercial skills – trustees who understand the importance of cashflow forecasting and so on. If you get that balance wrong then you will either struggle to understand your beneficiaries, or you will struggle to have enough money to help those beneficiaries.

3. Review the impact of your programmes

... if you are serious about cutting costs, you do need to spend some time assessing the viability of your various projects.

While this book is not about cutting projects, if you are serious about cutting costs, you do need to spend some time assessing the viability of your various projects. Does every programme you run produce the intended benefit? Does it help enough people? Does it succeed in getting the message across? Does it produce any worthwhile findings? Or is it just an expense that drains resources from the rest of the organisation? If it is little more than a cost, then you can cut it without any detrimental effect on the charity.

4. Avoid duplication with other charities

Check that you are not duplicating the work of another charity. If one of your campaigns is covering exactly the same ground as another charity, or if you offer a service that in effect competes with that offered by another charity, then you probably can save your organisation money by cutting that strand of your activity.

5. Merge with another organisation

Is there another charity which has a similar mission to you? Is there any overlap in the services that you offer, the campaigns you run or the messages you promote? If so, you could cut costs dramatically by merging.

As the credit crunch began to bite in late 2007, Help the Aged and Age Concern began merger talks for exactly this purpose, and the union of the two, very similar, organisations was completed about a year later.

A merger enables two organisations to make economies of scale on administration, fundraising and support functions, as well as in premises and facilities. If there is sufficient overlap between the two organisations then you can join forces, stop competing with each other, and deliver even more effectively on your mission.

Bear in mind that there will be many obstacles. Age Concern and Help the Aged had tried to merge three times in the previous decade, but talks had broken down each time. A major obstacle for those charities was the £13 million pension fund deficit that Age Concern England was carrying. However, other charities fall at other hurdles, such as the incompatibility of governance systems, lack of agreement on which previously competing projects to close, and very often, the egos of those at the top.

If you can put your ego to one side, find a suitable organisation and work hard to bring your charities together, it can be highly beneficial – not only for both organisations, but also for the cause you both support.

If you can put your ego to one side, find a suitable organisation, and work hard to bring your charities together, it can be highly beneficial...

6. Put a plan in place

Cost-cutting is difficult. You will run into opposition at every step, you will find yourself spending weeks introducing a cost-cutting plan only to find that it saves you much less than you expected, and you will have to fight hard for every single penny that you save your charity.

You need to find ways of keeping yourself motivated during those tough times. A great way of doing that is to have a long-term plan. Once you have picked up some

You need to find ways of keeping yourself motivated during those tough times.

ideas from this book, work out now how much you want to save in a year. Then, detail exactly how you will do that. Decide which of the ideas in this book you will put into practice, when you will do it, and how much you hope to save through each one.

Break down your plan into monthly and weekly goals. Take time every week to check your progress and amend your strategy as necessary. As you achieve each of your goals, physically cross them off your list, and keep a running total of how much money you are saving your charity.

Then, when five months from now, on a cold, dark Tuesday afternoon, you leave a staff meeting worried that none of your colleagues understands or even cares about your ideas, and convinced that you will never be able to put any real dent in the costs of your charity, take a look at your plan. You will be able to see how many ideas you have turned into reality, and exactly how much money you have saved your organisation. It will keep you motivated and will reinvigorate your enthusiasm for further cost-cutting.

7. Be realistic

...aim to make a small step forward every day.

Most of us tend to overestimate what we can achieve in a day and underestimate what we can achieve in a year. Do not set yourself unrealistic daily cost-cutting targets that dispirit you. Instead, aim to make a small step forward every day. In 365 days of small steps forward, you will be amazed at how far you have come.

8. Be ruthless in cutting non-core activity

Every charity has a core activity of what it does best. This will be some special expertise in that activity which means that it can help people, raise awareness of an issue, generate funding, conduct research into an area and so on, more cost-effectively than any other organisation. If this is not the case, then there is little reason for the organisation to continue to exist.

However, as time goes on, most charities expand and take on non-core activities. These are usually complementary to the core activity, using skills, knowledge and experience to operate in this new area. It is right and proper that successful organisations should expand to take on greater responsibility, but it can get to the point where an initially cost-effective organisation has taken on so many non-core activities that it is no longer efficient.

So, spend some time analysing your charity's activities. What is its core activity? Which non-core activities does it perform efficiently, and which less so? Then, be ruthless: cut the inefficient activities. This will allow you not only to focus your energies on the core activities at which you excel, it also will allow other organisations to move into the space that you occupied and operate there more efficiently than you did.

...focus your energies on the core activities at which you excel...

The process can be painful, but in the long run everyone wins.

9. Look to the long term

Mary Reilly, partner and head of the charities unit at accountancy firm Deloitte, advises charities both large and small on ways to cut costs. She offers this advice:

Always keep an eye on the long-term costs. It can be easy to just chip away at the easy stuff, making short-term gains but actually in the long run having very little significant impact on the organisation's finances. Don't be afraid to tackle the more difficult, strategic issues. They can be contentious, they usually involve a great deal of hard work, but very often it is getting these right that results in the long-term transformation of a charity's finances.

Don't be afraid to tackle the more difficult, strategic issues.

5

10. Don't assume you can do it alone

Lung diseases are Britain's second biggest killer, and the British Lung Foundation is the only charity in the UK that funds research into the prevention, diagnosis, treatment and cure of them. This vital work is funded entirely from voluntary contributions, so every penny which can be released from the overheads of running the charity counts towards finding a cure.

With this in mind, the British Lung Foundation engaged a consultancy firm called Expense Reduction Analysts to review expenditure on stationery and computer consumables. This resulted in a 36 per cent saving simply by changing supplier. Expense Reduction Analysts undertook the full review, from data collection through to tendering and implementation, liaising with Debbie Whatt, head of finance, throughout the project.

Whatt says: 'I was surprised by the savings identified by Expense Reduction Analysts as I had previously thought we were obtaining good prices. I'd already negotiated a 40 per cent discount from our existing stationery supplier.'

Don't be too proud to bring in help from colleagues, consultants and peers.

The lesson from this story is never to believe that you alone can find the maximum savings possible. Don't be too proud to bring in help from colleagues, consultants and peers.

11. Get a grant to help with your merger planning

The Government frequently offers grants to encourage the voluntary sector to become more efficient. For example, in 2009 it established a fund designed to help charities merge. The £16.5 million Modernisation Fund, which comprises loans and grants, is part of the Government's £42.5 million Third-Sector Action Plan, which sets out to help the sector survive the recession.

Charities with income of more than £750,000 are able to apply to Futurebuilders (www.futurebuilders-england. org.uk) for loans of between £30,000 and £500,000 to help them facilitate mergers. No interest is payable for up to five years, and repayment holidays for the first year may be granted. The application window opened in April 2009 and will remain open for a year.

Those with turnover of less than £1 million can contact Capacitybuilders (www.capacitybuilders.org.uk) to access grants. It will help them to access business support to explore the benefits of merger, collaboration or restructuring, and to meet the costs associated with these activities.

Chapter 2

Salaries

12. Know the total cost of employing someone

...the number one cost is salaries. Therefore, this should be the first area that you tackle.

For most charities – in fact, for most organisations of any type – the number one cost is salaries. Therefore, this should be the first area that you tackle. Even if you can make small percentage reductions in this area, you can cut your costs by thousands of pounds.

The first step should be to gain a clear picture of what each member of staff costs you and how much it costs you to hire each additional employee. On top of salaries, you need to make employer National Insurance contributions and pay for equipment such as a desk, computer and phone line, as well as any benefits that you offer.

Before you can start to cut any costs, you need to know exactly what these costs are. So start now. Write it down. You might be unpleasantly surprised by how much these employees are costing your charity.

13. Make sure all your staff are essential

This book is not about cutting costs by firing staff and cancelling fundraising initiatives. That is almost always the beginning of the end for any organisation. However, you do have a responsibility to check that everyone who receives a salary (and all those additional costs) is entirely essential to the operation and development of the organisation.

Take time to evaluate the contribution of each individual and the importance of each role. Remember to separate the two. Just because someone is not contributing, do not assume that the role is not necessary. It may be that you need to put a new person in that role.

Take time to evaluate the contribution of each individual and the importance of each role.

However, it might well be that you can make people redundant without any detrimental effect on the charity. Never rush into this – mistakes are extremely costly to rectify – but at the end of the day you cannot afford to be wasting resources on people who are not essential to the work of your charity.

14. Avoid duplicating roles

Spend some time looking at what your staff actually do every day. Is there any overlap between what they are doing? Look closely enough and the chances are that you will find at least one example of two people doing the same task. Find it, allocate it to one person, and make sure that the other person does something more useful.

A good way to start this is to ask each of your staff for a description of their responsibilities and duties. Not only will this allow you to spot any overlap very quickly and easily, it also will enable you to see which members of staff have a clear understanding of what they should be doing.

15. Ditch expensive staff

If you need to reduce your headcount, axe your senior, experienced staff before your junior, inexperienced ones. It might sound counter-intuitive, but consider these points:

- senior staff are paid highly, based on what they have achieved in the past

- you want staff who have the potential to achieve in the future
- if you can find that potential in someone who is just beginning their career, it will cost you much less than it will in someone who has years of experience.

You want staff who have the potential to achieve in the future.

If you do find yourself in the difficult situation of having to let someone go, remember that your junior staff are usually your cheapest staff. Of course, this should not be the only factor you consider, but it is something to bear in mind.

16. Keep overtime under control

Before you rush into laying off staff, consider the alternatives. When you are staring at a balance sheet littered with minus figures and red print, it might not seem like there are many options – but there are. With a bit of creative thinking and a lot of teamwork, you can keep the same headcount and cut your costs.

With a bit of creative thinking and a lot of teamwork, you can keep the same headcount and cut your costs.

Begin with looking at overtime. Paying staff overtime rates is wasteful. It is far better to plan ahead and allocate resources effectively so that you only pay people at their standard rates. Look back at when and where you have had to pay overtime rates in the past three months, and then look ahead to minimise this in the next three months. Review the situation in a further three months, so that you continuously refine your resource allocation.

17. Work out who is absolutely essential

When you get down to it, only two types of employee are actually essential for a charity to function: those who deliver the charity's mission and those who raise the funds to make it possible. The larger your organisation, the more types of staff you will need, and the more administrators there will be.

They probably do important work but is it essential? In today's age of computers, mobile phones and personal digital assistants, there is little need for administration staff. While 20 years ago every department had at least one secretary, and every senior executive had a personal assistant, today it is difficult to justify these expenses in the commercial sector, much less the voluntary sector. So, review your expenditure on administrative staff, and be prepared to make tough decisions.

. . . review your expenditure on administrative staff, and be prepared to make tough decisions.

18. Replace staff with volunteers

As a charity, your organisation has at least one major advantage over other organisations. Commercial organisations may be able to make huge profits, and public sector bodies may enjoy government subsidies, but neither of them have what you have: an army of committed and passionate volunteers.

It might be an exaggeration to describe them as an army. It might be only a handful, and they might need a bit of encouragement to show their commitment and passion. However, the fact still remains that your work is benefiting society in some way – you are doing more than making money or enforcing legislation – and because of this, you will find people who are willing to give up their time for free to help you achieve your goal.

So, make use of them. Whenever you lose a paid member of staff, do not immediately look to replace them with another person on the payroll. Think instead about whether a volunteer could take on the job.

You will need to ensure that the volunteer will have the skills, knowledge, time and commitment necessary. It might take an initial investment in training. You may need to split the role between several volunteers, and not every role can be done by volunteers. However, by making the most of this unique advantage, you may find that you can cut your wage bill considerably.

19. Lease your staff out

If times get really tough, you might have to consider letting some of your staff go. This is distressing to those losing their jobs, to those having to break the news, and to everyone left behind. Furthermore, if the good times do return, you might have to re-hire people for that position all over again.

One solution is to lease your staff to other organisations.

One far more positive solution is to lease your staff to other organisations. Say you need to save £10,000 in the next year: find a charity that needs a part-time fundraiser, and lease out half the time of your fundraiser who earns £20,000 a year. Not only will you make your cost saving, but your employee will gain a fresh perspective on their work, and everyone will be pleased that you avoided having to let someone go.

20. Link pay to performance

In the private and public sectors, pay is linked increasingly to performance. Why should it be different in the voluntary sector? Of course, it might not be possible to link everyone's pay to performance, and it might not be desirable in every case. However, you will find that by giving certain staff clear objectives, and making a proportion of their pay dependent upon the achievement of those goals, you can improve their productivity and ensure that your organisation is not paying people for something that they are not doing.

Do this correctly, and you will find that you improve the morale of those staff. Everyone likes to feel that they are doing a good job, and the only way they can know whether or not they are performing well is to receive clear objectives. The only way to make those goals meaningful is to link them to pay. However, do it incorrectly and you could alienate and demotivate your staff.

Bear these points in mind:

- targets need to be fair and mutually agreed
- you must give staff the chance to perform outstandingly well and so earn more than they already do
- communication is key: keep staff well informed, and present this not as a cost-cutting exercise but as an opportunity for them
- introduce performance-related pay gradually, allowing people to get used to it over time.

... give staff the chance to perform outstandingly well and so earn more than they already do.

21. Offer holidays instead of pay

Many people value holiday time more than income, so think about offering new recruits more holiday time and less pay. Give existing staff the option of a pay cut in return for more time off. Be careful, however, that in doing this you do not leave your organisation understaffed at any point.

22. Make full-time jobs part time

How many people in your organisation would prefer to work part time? This could involve giving them Fridays off, or allowing them to arrive late and leave early to fit in around the school run. Would this really affect their output for the organisation? If you look closely, you might well be able to find people who could work effectively part time, who you could pay commensurately less – and all without any detrimental effect on the work of your charity.

If you look closely, you might well be able to find people who could work effectively part time ...

23. Freeze pay for a year

Another alternative to making one or two people redundant is to introduce a pay freeze. Employees tend to expect an annual pay rise, usually a little above the rate of inflation. The charity gets no more productivity out of those staff for that automatic pay rise, so consider how much you could save by not providing it. Would it mean that you could avoid making someone redundant?

... consider how much you could save by not providing an automatic pay rise.

Put the question to your staff. Would they accept a pay freeze for a year – or even a slight reduction in salary, to be refunded to them when income picks up again – if it meant that no one had to be made redundant in the next six months?

Most people would understand that this is an unfortunate but necessary alternative to redundancy. It might be unpopular and painful, but if the whole sector is struggling, staff will be unlikely to find alternative employment elsewhere, and you will keep your most capable and committed employees. You will be glad of them when the good times return.

24. Use the Probation Service to fill vacancies

CIRCA (Centre for Information, Resource, Care and Assistance) is a charity based on the Isle of Man which has been placing probationers successfully in voluntary work for the past 15 months. Not only has this done a great deal to improve the job prospects of ex-offenders, it also has provided many local charities with essential voluntary labour.

The partnership is not linked to any punishment, court order or community service. All work is undertaken on a purely voluntary basis. Probationers can make use of existing skills, or learn new ones in roles such as administration, social care or manual labour.

The scheme is not just operating on the Isle of Man. Sarah Thorn, fundraising manager at Bath Cats and Dogs Home, says:

> We like to think we leave no stone unturned in our ongoing efforts to cut costs. So we've recently started using the Probation Service to fill vacancies. They are providing volunteers that can help in the home with the animals, with maintenance and in the office. We have only just started using them, but they should keep wage costs down.

25. Increase the hours your staff work

New staff are expensive. You have to pay for recruitment fees or advertisements, you have to spend time and money training them up, and you have to provide them with a space to work and equipment such as a PC and phone. So, next time you need to hire someone, consider increasing the hours of your existing employees instead.

You may be imagining how your team will react, picturing picket lines and organisational chaos. Well, that does not have to be the outcome.

...next time you need to hire someone, consider increasing the hours of your existing employees instead.

Consider offering to pay them more for the extra hours. The extra you pay them still should be less than the new employee would cost – especially when you take into account the add-on costs of an extra employee – and because your existing staff already know the job, they will be able to get more work done in less time than someone new.

Explain to your staff that you need more resource in the department, and outline how much it will cost the organisation to recruit, train and house a new person. For example, their salary will be £12,000 a year, recruitment will cost £1,000, training £1,000 and other costs £2,000 a year so this makes £16,000.

Then suggest that instead, the team share this extra workload between them in return for the salary of £12,000. If there are 12 in the department, then they need to do roughly an extra three hours a week each, or start 20 minutes earlier and end 20 minutes later. They receive a pay rise of £1,000 a year. You save £4,000.

In this way, you can present the proposal to your employees as a pay rise for increased responsibility across the board. Far from being up in arms about it, they might be very much in favour.

26. Offer staff pensions rather than pay

...for a higher rate tax-payer, pension contributions are worth 40 per cent more than the equivalent salary.

One of the most tax-efficient ways of rewarding staff is through pension contributions. This is because the Government allows tax relief on employer contributions to registered pension schemes. So, for a higher rate tax-payer, pension contributions are worth 40 per cent more than the equivalent salary.

For a detailed employer's guide to company pension schemes, see: www.thepensionservice.gov.uk.

27. Overpay your best staff

Like most organisations, you probably have a handful of staff who are outstanding. They are more talented, more committed and more productive than their peers, and you probably wonder how you would cope without them. Every organisation has these people. They usually make up no more than 5 per cent of the workforce, and they are indeed absolutely critical to the continued success of your charity. So you should overpay them.

Overpay them? But this is a book about how to cut costs, isn't it?

Absolutely. You need to overpay these people by 10–20 per cent because, like any employee, if they leave it will cost you 10–20 per cent of their annual salary in recruitment, training and lost time. However, with these stars you also will lose that extra something that they bring to your organisation. In the long term, overpaying your top staff is the best way to save money for your charity.

. . . overpaying your top staff is the best way to save money for your charity.

28. Close the human resources department

While human resources (HR) professionals can add much to an organisation, they are also a non-essential overhead.

Of course, they can help to ensure that you hire the right staff, that those staff are properly trained and motivated, and that you are getting the most out of your people. They can provide expert advice on legal issues around disciplinary issues, and this can help to avoid employment tribunals.

However, if you really need to cut some costs then one fairly drastic answer is simply to close your HR department. Other people – possibly you – will be able to pick up the essential functions, and you will be able to supplement that with some consultants. You will be able to use free online resources such as www.personneltoday.com for much of the information and advice which your HR department might have provided.

It might not be pretty, but it certainly will improve your balance sheet.

It may be worth your while, however, having someone responsible for just the recruiting side of things: see tip 45.

Chapter 3

Benefits

29. Cut employee benefits

Employee benefits can be a significant cost for any organisation, and this is especially the case for charities. Over time, it can be easy for a charity to add minor benefits to employment packages. They are useful for attracting good staff, help you to keep your best staff, and each one on its own seems relatively inexpensive.

However, if you were to go through them all now and add them up, you might be shocked by how much money you are spending on them. Do they really make your organisation a more attractive place to work? Wouldn't the best staff stay there because they know they do a good job and enjoy being part of a team that is achieving so much?

Read the rest of this chapter, and then publicly make a cut in one of your benefits.

Cutting benefits is never going to be a popular move, and you will need to do it gradually and with sensitivity. By far the best place to start is with your own benefits. Set an example. Read the rest of this chapter, and then publicly make a cut in one of your benefits. Consider getting your trustees to do the same.

This will set an example, and will make your ensuing programme of benefit cutting much more palatable to those around you. Also, it will start the process of trimming your expenditure in this area.

30. Offer small, cheap incentives rather than large, expensive benefits

It might have become the norm for employers to offer their valued staff large, expensive benefits such as pensions, cars and health insurance. However, there is little evidence to suggest that these benefits do anything other than eat into an organisation's bottom line. The problem is that people tend to see them as part of their package and take them for granted, so they do little to motivate staff or make them more loyal to an employer.

If you want to create a positive atmosphere in the workplace, you might find it more effective to offer spontaneous, short-term rewards for specific actions. For example, offer a bottle of champagne to the fundraiser who signs up the most major donors in a week, or dinner for two to the employee who comes up with the best cost-saving idea of the month. Incentives such as these focus minds on a specific area, can be fun for those involved, and – best of all – are relatively inexpensive.

. . . offer spontaneous, short-term rewards for specific actions.

31. Let staff use office phones to make personal calls

A remarkable number of organisations expend great effort on preventing their staff from making personal phone calls from landlines during work hours. This is despite the fact that the calls themselves cost next to nothing, the management time spent sorting it out costs much more than the cost of the calls, the ill-will generated by these policies is detrimental to staff productivity, and often staff can sort out an issue, say with childcare, with one simple phone call that otherwise can take them away from work for half a day.

. . . often staff can sort out an issue with one simple phone call that otherwise can take them away from work.

In most cases, you will save money by relaxing this rule. Let staff know that they can make personal calls on office

19

lines, but that they should not abuse this benefit. Monitor this remotely, and only intervene if someone is blatantly taking advantage.

32. Stop staff using work mobiles to make personal calls

If your staff have mobile phones for business use, the personal calls they make on them can be expensive. Individually, these calls might add up to just a few pounds a month, but if you add them up across your entire team over a year, they are a significant cost. So make sure that employees have separate phones for personal calls.

If someone is making a large number of expensive calls outside of work hours, have a quiet word...

Let staff know that that is your policy, then monitor all bills closely for three months. If someone is making a large number of expensive calls outside of work hours, have a quiet word with them. You might choose to focus your initial efforts on the members of staff with the largest mobile bills.

33. Reduce holiday entitlement for new starters

Giving employees holiday is like giving money away. You are in effect paying them and getting nothing in return. Of course, staff are legally entitled to a certain number of days of annual leave, and even if you were able to end all holiday entitlement overnight you would probably lose all your staff almost as quickly. However, this does not mean that you cannot trim your costs by making sure that you are offering around the average number of holidays.

Giving employees holiday is like giving money away.

Do some research among comparable organisations in your area, simply by picking up the phone and asking your peers at those organisations. If you explain why you are calling, they probably will be happy to help. They will be just as interested to know what you are offering your staff.

If you discover that there is room to reduce holiday entitlement without damaging your recruitment prospects or your employee productivity levels, then change the entitlement of new starters. You cannot change employment terms for existing employees, but just by reducing it for new starters you can significantly reduce over time the amount of money that you give away through holidays.

34. Reduce redundancy payments

Redundancy payments were intended originally as a cushion for people who were losing jobs that they had done all their lives, and who lived in areas where there was very little prospect of alternative work. Miners in the 1980s needed generous redundancy payments, but by and large, office workers in the 2000s do not. Many of the people who work for you could walk into a new job tomorrow if you had to make them redundant. So, scrap over-generous redundancy payments and pay the statutory minimum.

Miners in the 1980s needed generous redundancy payments, but office workers in the 2000s by and large do not.

35. Put an end to 'away days'

In recent years the staff 'away day' has become ever more popular. From days at the races to kayaking in north Wales or even weekends skiing in the Alps, organisations both large and small, across all sectors, are all spending thousands of pounds on these events.

Proponents argue that getting away from the office allows participants to focus on training, strategy development or whatever it is they are meant to be doing. They argue that putting work colleagues in an unfamiliar setting can help them to work more effectively as a team back in the office.

However, there is precious little evidence to support any of these claims. There is certainly too little evidence to

If your staff want to go kayaking in Wales, let them spend their own money on it.

justify a cash-strapped charity spending any money on them. If your staff want to go to the races, or kayaking in Wales or skiing in the Alps, then let them spend their own money on it.

36. Scrap your employee assistance programme

Giving staff free access to a legal helpline, emergency childcare cover, counselling services and all the elements of an employee assistance programme can do a great deal to reduce absenteeism and increase productivity. However, it is also extremely expensive. Get rid of this cost, and instead provide your staff with the phone numbers and websites of free local agencies, such as the Citizens Advice Bureau, that will perform the same tasks.

37. End your defined-benefit pension scheme

Not so long ago, most people worked for the same employer for almost their entire careers and looked forward to a generous pension when they finally retired. These 'defined-benefit' pension schemes, where employees knew exactly what their pension would be when they retired, were incredibly expensive for those organisations to run. During times of poor stockmarket returns, they became a significant drain on the organisation's resources. However, almost every employer offered them. If an organisation wanted to attract and retain the top talent, it needed to provide one.

Then it all changed. In the 1980s, the employment market opened up considerably. People began to move jobs for higher salaries, a weakened trade union movement meant that companies no longer felt the need show loyalty to staff, and in return those staff began to think nothing of deserting their employers for the promise of higher wages elsewhere. The concept of a job for life was finished.

Then, in the stockmarket collapse of the early 1990s, those employers decided that they could no longer justify their generous defined benefit pension schemes for staff who were likely to move on within five years anyway. So, they closed the schemes. There are now almost no private sector employers offering these pensions. Most now offer stakeholder pensions, which are joint funded by the employee, the employer and the Government, and are much less expensive for employers.

Yet a remarkable number of charities still offer their staff these defined benefit pensions. If you are running one, you can save yourself thousands of pounds by closing it. You will meet fierce opposition, and you should be prepared for the impact on staff motivation and loyalty. However, that downside will be temporary. In the years to come you will notice no negative effect on employee recruitment or retention, and a vastly positive effect on your balance sheet.

If you are running a defined pension, you can save yourself thousands of pounds by closing it.

38. Offer recognition as an incentive

Some people only go to work to make money, but very few of them end up in the voluntary sector. Most of us are in it because we care about the work that we do, and we can see the chance to make a difference with the skills, experience and time that we have.

So, when a member of your team performs particularly well, why reward them with a pay rise or a bonus?

For many people, but especially those in the voluntary sector, it will mean a great deal more to be recognised for outstanding achievement than to have a few extra pounds every week. Introduce a way in which you can celebrate the achievements of your top performers. It could be an announcement at a monthly company meeting. It could

Introduce a way in which you can celebrate the achievements of your top performers.

23

be a plaque on the wall. Or it could just be a quiet word in your office. However you do it, find some ways of making it clear just how much you value their contribution.

It will be a more effective way of motivating them and retaining them, and it will cost a lot less.

39. Watch employee expenses like a hawk

GlobalExpense, the UK's largest employee expenses service provider, conducts an annual employee expenses benchmark report which is based on actual payments to employees. The 2009 report revealed that UK managers wrongly approve around £2 billion for employee expenses every year.

...an estimated £1.08 billion of fiddled expense claims are wrongly approved for payment.

It estimates that managers approve payments for 11 per cent of all employee expense claims (around £923 million) that should never be paid because the items purchased are not covered by company policy. On top of this, an estimated £1.08 billion of fiddled expense claims are wrongly approved for payment.

The 2009 report draws on more than 4.8 million expense claims from more than 150,000 UK-based employees resulting in more than £270 million in payments to employees during 2007 and 2008.

Claims outside company policy in 2008 included: handcuffs, a bribe to border guards to get out of Iraq, nine personal massages charged to a hotel bill because the claimant had had 'a really stressful day', renewing a passport and, remarkably, condoms. The largest single paid expense claim was £38,179, as compensation for a cancelled holiday.

2008 was not an unsual year. It is a sad fact that a small percentage of employees will always try to get away with whatever they can, so you need to make sure that they do not succeed.

Introducing stricter policies on what employees can and cannot claim for is not enough. You need to police the system. You must begin by training all managers who authorise expense payments so they know when to challenge a claim.

Your next step will be to monitor big spenders. According to GlobalExpense, almost 30 per cent of employees received more than £1,500 in expenses in 2008 and 15 per cent of individual claims were for £100 or more. GlobalExpense research shows that 30 per cent of employees think that it is fine to exaggerate expense claims. You need to identify the big claimers in your organisation, and make sure that their claims are closely scrutinised.

...30 per cent of employees think that it is fine to exaggerate expense claims.

40. Offer childcare vouchers

Bear in mind that some benefits can help you to save money. For example, the childcare voucher scheme is a government-backed initiative introduced to help working parents cope with the spiralling cost of childcare. At the time of writing, the scheme allows businesses to provide employees with up to £55 worth of vouchers per week (£243 per month or £2,916 per year), which can be used to pay for any type of registered or approved childcare for youngsters up to age 16.

These vouchers are advantageous for working parents because they are free of tax and National Insurance contributions, and can save each parent up to £1,195 per year. Meanwhile, employers running childcare voucher schemes also reap the benefits, saving up to 12.8 per cent (£373 per employee, per year), in National Insurance savings alone.

(For up-to-date figures and information, see: www.inland revenue.gov.uk/childcare or call the Employers' Helpline on 08457 143143.)

Chapter 4

Recruitment

41. Retain your good staff

New staff are expensive. Even before they have joined your company, they cost a great deal to recruit. When you take into account advertising costs, management time, induction and training costs, each new person you hire costs an average of £5,000.

Keeping your existing staff always should be a priority.

Keeping your existing staff always should be a priority. Of course, this only applies to good staff. If someone is underperforming, you need to work with them to give them the skills, knowledge, confidence and motivation to perform well. If they are still failing, you need to let them go and find a replacement.

However, for the great majority of your employees this will not be the case. They will be good, committed members of the team who make your organisation what it is. You need to manage them well so that they enjoy working at your charity and continue to do so.

Give them clear targets and objectives. Communicate with them frequently and openly. Listen to their concerns, treat them with respect, and address all genuine concerns. Give them a vision of the future – show them where they will be in 10 years' time, where the organisation will be, and what you will all have achieved during that time together.

This combination of simple good management and inspiring leadership will slash your recruitment costs.

42. Avoid recruitment mistakes

The high cost of recruitment means you need to avoid making recruitment mistakes. When you consider the opportunities that your organisation will miss out on through not having the right person in the post for weeks or months – to say nothing of the potential damage to your organisation's reputation – it soon becomes clear that establishing a rigorous and effective selection process is absolutely essential.

43. Implement a one-year recruitment freeze

People cost money. Recruiting people costs money. A simple way of reducing your outgoings is to put a freeze on all recruitment for a certain amount of time – say a year.

You will meet opposition. If existing staff say that they cannot handle the workload and need an extra pair of hands to help out, you might find it cost-effective to pay them a little more to work a little longer and harder than to hire a new full-time member of staff. This sort of pay rise usually quells most objections to a recruitment freeze.

However, be careful when you unfreeze recruitment. Often this is seen as the time to recruit all the people that the organisation would have brought on board during the freeze. Recruiters become overloaded, and you end up paying more for agencies than you would if you had spread the recruitment out normally. To ensure that this does not happen, make it clear when you restart normal levels of recruitment that they are just that – normal – and there is no need to 'play catch-up'.

. . . establishing a rigorous and effective selection process is absolutely essential.

. . . make it clear when you restart normal levels of recruitment that they are just that – normal . . .

44. Identify key positions, and fill only those

An alternative to an outright recruitment freeze is to recruit only for key positions. Work out which roles need to be filled in order for your charity to function. Then, if an incumbent leaves one of those positions, fill it, but if someone leaves another position, do not fill it. This more moderate approach can allow you to keep a longer freeze on non-essential positions. However, bear in mind that while they may not be essential, many roles are important, so only freeze recruitment for as long as necessary.

45. Make someone responsible for recruitment

Hiring the right staff is important to any organisation, so most have standardised selection procedures. If a line manager wants to hire someone, they use an application form and interviews, and adhere to generally agreed selection criteria. This ensures a consistent approach across the organisation.

Yet very often, the very organisations that are so consistent in selection procedures will take an entirely ad hoc approach to recruitment. Each line manager will book their own recruitment advertisements, or will negotiate their own deals with recruitment agencies. This is wasteful.

... appoint one person to head up recruitment.

All you need to do is appoint one person to head up recruitment. They can negotiate centralised deals with recruitment advertisers and agencies. With their bulk purchasing power they should be able to get good discounts, and they can make sure that no part of your organisation is paying well over the odds.

46. Fill job vacancies without spending a penny on recruitment

When we have a job vacancy, very often the first thing we do is rush out, buy some advertising space and write an advertisement. Or we might even hire a recruitment consultant. However, before you jump into this process, always consider internal candidates.

Look at your current staff and ask if any of them could do this job. Not only will it save you time and money, but you will not need to worry about whether or not they will fit into your organisation. Furthermore, often you can generate resentment if you fail to consider promotion before recruitment. So think hard before spending money on those recruitment advertisements.

... think hard before spending money on those recruitment advertisements.

47. Do your own headhunting

Headhunting is a great way of recruiting senior staff, but it is too expensive for most charities even to consider. Headhunters generally ask for 25 per cent of the employee's first-year salary, which, if you are hiring someone on £40,000, is an eye-watering £10,000. However, this does not mean that you should give up on headhunting altogether. With a bit of effort you can simply do it yourself.

Start by compiling a list of the people you know who might fit your brief. Do not limit this to staff at other charities. Think about the skills required to do the job, and brainstorm ideas about positions in other organisations that would require those skills. Think of people you met at industry events, or those you have read about or have heard speak. Ask colleagues and acquaintances if they know anyone who might be good for the job.

Ask colleagues and acquaintances if they know anyone who might be good for the job.

29

Once you have a few potential candidates, you need to call them and try to sell them the job. However, this does not mean making obtrusive, pushy calls to people: that will do more to deter potential employees and damage your reputation. Instead, focus on getting to know this individual, and on starting a long-term relationship.

Call outside of work hours, ideally on a mobile phone, and introduce yourself immediately, telling them honestly why you are calling. You might find that some will refuse to talk to you, but don't be put off by those rejections. You are not doing anything wrong, and you are likely to find that on the contrary, most people will feel complimented and will be very happy to talk to you.

Your focus then should be on getting them to talk about themselves. Before the call, find out as much about them as you can, so that you have plenty of material to engage them in conversation. If the conversation goes well, suggest a relaxed chat over a coffee to explore mutual opportunities.

If they agree, you have just successfully headhunted someone! You still have to interview them, and it may not translate into a cost-free hire, but at least you have piqued their interest without spending thousands of pounds on headhunters. If it does not work out, maintain the relationship anyway – you never know what opportunities might arise in the future.

... pause, think carefully about exactly what sort of person you need in this role, and get it down in writing ...

48. Write clear job specifications

All too often we rush into recruitment. We see a job that needs to be filled, so we immediately post a job advertisement or get on the phone to the recruitment agency. Before doing that, it always pays to pause, think carefully about exactly what sort of person you need in this role, and get it down in writing as a job specification. This should detail:

- why this role is important to the organisation
- what specific responsibilities and tasks will be associated with the role
- which qualities will make someone successful at the role.

Avoid making the mistake of simply describing the previous occupant of the role. They may have done the job brilliantly, but there is a reason they are not doing it any more. The organisation has probably changed, and the demands of the role will have shifted accordingly. You might need an entirely different type of person now.

In the same way, try to look forwards rather than backwards when describing the type of person you want. Qualifications and experience are important, but they are not as important as attitude and potential. Very often we hire on experience and fire on attitude. So take time to write down the personality traits and attitudes that you believe will be essential to success in this role.

. . . often we hire on experience and fire on attitude.

49. Interview effectively

The interview is the most important element of the selection process, yet it is the most difficult to get right. It can be hard to be objective, and many interviewers struggle to strike the right balance between selling the job and assessing the interviewee.

Preparation can help. Work out beforehand what you will ask candidates, make sure the questions relate directly to the skills and qualities required in the role, ask all candidates the same questions, and consider using a scoring system for all.

A successful interview is one in which you will be talking very little. Ask candidates open questions that will encourage them to tell you about their experience, motivation and future goals. People prefer talking to

A successful interview is one in which you will be talking very little.

31

listening, and it will give you a chance to listen carefully to what they're saying.

Finally, don't ignore entirely how well you get on with the candidate. It is likely that you will have to work very closely with this individual, so it is important that you get on well with each other.

50. Use psychometric testing

Psychometric testing takes the form of face-to-face discussions or online questionnaires that provide information about predicted behaviour in different circumstances. The findings can be used to indicate a person's aptitude for certain activities and how they would react in a working environment.

Psychometric tests have a bad reputation in many quarters, but they can be an excellent way of removing subjective bias from a selection process. In fact, it is mostly candidates who don't like them – for recruiters they are a very useful tool.

Psychometric tests could prevent you from wasting thousands of pounds in recruiting the wrong people.

They will cost you money, but probably less than you think and, used together with effective interviews, could prevent you from wasting thousands of pounds in recruiting the wrong people. A simple online search will lead you to the website of the leading providers of these tests.

51. Always take up references

Hiring the wrong person can cost your organisation thousands of pounds. Someone may have a sparkling CV, may sail through every interview, and may appear to be exactly what you are looking for to fill a vacancy. However, before you rush to bring them on board, always take up references.

52. Cut the size of your recruitment advertisements

If someone is looking for a job at an organisation such as yours, they will look at the vacancies pages of the publications where you advertise. They will scan them fairly carefully. After all, that's what you would do if you were looking, wouldn't you? You wouldn't just skim it, pausing only to read the larger advertisements.

Good candidates who are serious about finding a new job will take the time to read every job advertisement, no matter how small. So why should you pay more for larger advertisements? Next time you are recruiting, try a smaller advertisement and see if it affects your response.

Next time you are recruiting, try a smaller advertisement...

53. Post job advertisements online

Job advertisements can be expensive. That is why more and more organisations are using websites such as Gumtree (www.gumtree.com) to post advertisements. It is popular with overseas visitors to the UK and – best of all – it is entirely free to post an advertisement.

However, depending on the type of work they do, some charities also use job advertisements as a more strategic marketing tool within the sector to increase awareness of their organisation. If this is the case consider advertising on some of the sites run by charity umbrella bodies which offer low-cost recruitment advertising. See British Overseas NGOs for Development (www.bond.org.uk), the London Voluntary Service Council (www.lvsc.org.uk) or the National Council for Voluntary Agencies job shop (www.ncvo-jobshop.org.uk).

...try advertising on some of the sites run by charity umbrella bodies...

54. Move your recruitment advertisements online

You probably use industry publications and local newspapers for much of your recruitment advertising. Potential recruits know to look there, and the system has worked well for many years. However, more and more of these titles are developing online versions that do away with printing costs and attract readers with high-quality editorial. Importantly for you, advertising on these web versions tends to be a fair bit cheaper than the print equivalent. Why not put in a call to the advertising sales team and see how much you could save by moving your recruitment advertising online?

... advertising on web versions tends to be a fair bit cheaper than the print equivalent.

55. Offer a finder's fee to staff

One of the best sources of potential new recruits is your existing staff. The chances are that they will have friends and family who are similar to them. They also know what it is like to work at your organisation, so can give their friend or relative a good idea of whether or not they would like working there.

Offer to pay staff 20 per cent of what you would normally pay a recruitment agency ...

Using your staff can work out significantly cheaper than recruitment advertisements and agencies. Offer to pay them 20 per cent of what you would normally pay a recruitment agency and watch them spring into action!

56. Ask your suppliers to recruit for you

Your suppliers are likely to work for similar organisations, so they may know many people who would be ideal employees for you. Why not email them a monthly list of vacancies in your organisation, asking them if they have any ideas of possible candidates? They are not only ideally placed to help you, they also have a great incentive to do so, and are unlikely to expect payment for their help.

57. Recruit through local schools, colleges and universities

Schools, colleges and universities are full of bright, enthusiastic people who not only need a first step on the career ladder but also would love the chance to work at a charity. Contact local academic institutions and tell them about your vacancies. Offer to go and speak at a careers event. Ask when graduate recruitment fairs are being held, and see if you can book a stand there.

Contact local academic institutions and tell them about your vacancies.

58. Use Student Gems to recruit students

Student Gems is a website that connects employers with students. You can post details of the work that you need doing, and students respond explaining why they would be well suited to help with your project. The students get great work experience and earn some money. You may need to supervise them closely at first, but you should be able to find an intelligent and motivated person who will work for a relatively low hourly rate. (See: www.student gems.com.)

59. Take on apprentices

There are already more than 400,000 apprentices in businesses across the UK, and the Government is investing more than £1 billion over the coming years to increase the number of apprentice places in the UK. Offering an apprenticeship can be an affordable way of bringing extra resource into your organisation. It also gives you the opportunity to develop an employee who knows your charity inside out and is keen to repay you for giving them a start on the career ladder.

Offering an apprenticeship can be an affordable way of bringing extra resource into your organisation.

35

Find out more about taking on an apprentice either by visiting the website of the Learning and Skills Council at: www.apprenticeships.org.uk/wanttoemployanapprentice or by calling for a free information pack on 0800 150400.

60. Use CSV to recruit volunteers

If you spend money recruiting volunteers, have you looked into how Community Service Volunteers (CSV) could help? Founded in 1962, CSV aims to involve young people aged 16–35 in voluntary service in the UK with a view to enriching their lives, and those they help, as well as generating social change.

... CSV has an enormous army of volunteers which your organisation could be using.

CSV is the UK's largest volunteering and training charity. In 2008 it helped nearly a quarter of a million people to volunteer in the UK, and it continues to do so every year. That is an enormous army of volunteers which your organisation could be using. Get in touch with your local CSV (www.csv.org.uk) and ask how they can help you.

Chapter 5

Training

61. Invest in training

Training matters. If you don't train your staff and volunteers, they will lack the skills and knowledge that they need to do their jobs. Therefore, cutting investment in training can be a false economy, as without capable staff you will have to redo tasks, and you will spend more time firefighting problems than making progress.

A recent report by the Cranfield School of Management revealed that organisations which invest in their staff are 44 per cent more likely to save money than those that offer no formal or ad hoc training. Despite this, only 34 per cent of businesses have a formal training strategy in place.

The lesson is clear: no matter how tough times get, resist the temptation to halt all training, and keep investing in your people.

Cutting investment in training can be a false economy...

62. Don't assume that training is the answer

In too many organisations, buying in training is a knee-jerk reaction. When something does not work as well as it should, we assume that this indicates a training need. While this is in many ways a commendable attitude, and is far better than assuming it is a result of employee indolence or malign external forces, it can lead to overspending on unnecessary training.

Before rushing in to buy training, look at what changes you can make through job design or employee reward, or just by setting up a meeting to discuss the problem. Very often you will find that the solution is simpler and cheaper than training. This is not to undermine the importance of developing your staff – it is more about recognising that development is about more than just training.

63. Prioritise the urgent training needs

Work out which training courses are essential and which are merely desirable…

Training is often an easy area in which to make cuts. However, buying in good training is one of the cheapest ways of keeping staff motivated, engaged and productive. It is far cheaper than increasing salaries. So, instead of making cuts, prioritise the most urgent training needs.

Work out which training courses are essential and which are merely desirable, basing your decisions on your organisation's overall objectives and needs. For example, is fundraising a key priority? Then focus training budgets on building skills and knowledge in that area. Perhaps you are aiming for major grant awards? Then send your staff on courses that will make their tenders as compelling as possible. Or if you are looking to cut costs, financial management is probably a priority, so buy in training in that area.

64. Share existing knowledge within your organisation

…think about what skills already exist within your organisation.

Be smart about where you invest your training budget. Before you spend a penny on external training courses, think about the skills that already exist within your organisation. Who is an expert in PowerPoint? Who looked after invoicing in a previous job? Who always manages to build strong relationships with corporate partners? Who knows your region's grant-making system inside out?

Throughout your organisation there will be a vast array of skills. You might not be aware of them, so ask people what they are good at doing, then set up a system for staff to share their skills and knowledge with everyone else in the organisation. For example, run a weekly lunchtime seminar in which one person presents to their colleagues on their specialist topic, rotated so that the burden is shared and the learning as varied as possible. Imagine how much everyone could learn in a year. Imagine how much that could trim from your training budget.

65. Share knowledge with other organisations

As well as using the existing knowledge within your organisation, look at what knowledge exists in other organisations that you know. Whatever your training need, there may be someone at one of your suppliers, or at a neighbouring business, charity or government body, who can meet it.

... look at what knowledge exists in other organisations you know.

Organisations with which you work in partnership should be very keen to help you in this way. From their point of view, sending you a member of their team for a few hours is a great way to cement their relationship with you. Meanwhile, you could save thousands of pounds. Other organisations might need more persuasion, but you might be able to set up reciprocal arrangements. Why not pick up the phone now, or send an email, and see if you can save money on external training courses in this way?

66. Set up job swaps

Short-term job swaps can be an excellent way of developing your employees' skills and bringing fresh expertise into your organisation for a period of time. They also cost nothing, apart from the time that it takes to run them.

To set one up, you need to find an organisation which has a complementary need, and staff who are willing to endure the disruption for a few weeks or months. This can be a challenge, but those who do try the experience usually end up enthused by the different perspective that it gives them and the new contacts they have made, and invigorated by the change to their routine. Try putting some feelers out to local employers and among your staff.

...find an organisation which has a complementary need and staff who are willing to endure disruption...

67. Seek grant-funded training

There is a vast array of grant-funded training available for voluntary sector organisations. Ask peers in other charities if they know of any funding for which you might be eligible. Contact training providers and simply ask what grant-funded training they have available. Take a look at the website www.fit4funding.org.uk – it is a charity that helps other charities to access funding.

Ask peers if they know of any funding for which you might be eligible.

The Directory of Social Change (DSC) aims to help small and medium-sized organisations receive the training that they need, and one of the main ways in which it achieves this is through grant-funded training programmes. For example, in 2007 and early 2008 it ran a trustee development programme aimed at providing new and potential trustees from the black and minority ethnic and the mental health sectors with the skills and knowledge to become effective trustees. In 2009 it is running 'Getting a fair deal from contracts' – a three-day introductory programme for managers and trustees involved in bidding for, negotiating and managing contracts and service agreements.

(To see what grant-funded training DSC currently is running, go to: www.dsc.org.uk.)

68. Approach your suppliers for free training

Ask suppliers such as your accountant, your IT contractor and your recruitment agents if they will run any free seminars to which you could go along. For them, this is an inexpensive way to recruit and retain clients, while for you it is an excellent, low-cost way to keep up to date with developments in a key area of your work.

Ask suppliers if they will run any free seminars to which you could go along.

For example, Enable Interactive is a Bristol-based digital marketing agency which has worked for charities such as Breast Cancer Care, WWF, British Red Cross and War Child, as well as for brands such as Clarks, Microsoft and Channel 4. It regularly runs free digital workshops for charities.

> *Over the years we've amassed incredible knowledge of the not-for-profit sector: how charities work, how people respond to their marketing and communications and most importantly, what success looks like,' explains Matt Connolly, Enable's strategy director. 'With the economy as it is at the moment, charities need to rethink the way that they communicate with their audiences. Enable is in an excellent position to lead the way on this and help charities get considerably more return for their investment and build for the future.*

The format of the workshops is simple: in an open dialogue with the charity's team, Enable shares the learning gained from past projects, and looks at digital trends and what opportunities they can bring for that organisation, as well as the role that digital can play in a charity's marketing and fundraising plans and how it can maximise its future potential.

Ben Akin-Smith, Enable's head of planning, explains:
> *One of our key findings is that, on the whole, individual donations are not decreasing – it's just that people don't want to give to new charities. What is impacting most,*

41

however, is that legacy donation is massively down – this could be due to people redirecting their donation, but most likely because the value of their assets is so depressed. Either way, it presents a big problem to charities, one that further increases the importance of effective marketing and communications – and that's where digital can help.

69. Request free passes to conferences

Conferences offer you the opportunity to learn about many subjects and interact with a large number of people, all in a condensed time frame and place, but they can be expensive. Try asking for charity discounts, waiting for last-minute deals, or volunteering to speak in return for one or two free passes.

Try volunteering to speak in return for free passes.

70. 'Piggyback' on local authority training

Local authorities operate comprehensive training programmes for their staff. Your local authority might be willing to let you send your staff on its training programmes at a discounted rate or free of charge – especially if you already work with them.

71. Find training and funding through Train to Gain

Train to Gain was launched by the Learning and Skills Council (LSC) to help the UK plug the skills gap with its main rivals such as Germany, France and the United States. For you, this means free government support to train your staff.

If you contact Train to Gain (www.traintogain.gov.uk), a broker will visit your business and carry out a free training needs analysis. They will put you in touch with suitable training providers, and source any available funding. In addition, if you have fewer than 50 full-time employees, you may be eligible for a contribution to your wage costs for staff while they are training.

With the opening of its new Gorilla Kingdom attraction, London Zoo was anticipating a busy year in 2007. The thousands of extra visitors would put staff under the spotlight. Excellent customer service is always vital to the zoo's success, but at that time in particular human resources manager Karen Turnbull wanted to raise the general standard of skills and qualifications among staff, ensuring that every visitor received a consistently high standard of service. Turnbull says:

> *Staff working in customer-facing roles such as catering or retail are the public face of the zoo. It's really important that they have the best possible training. It's also important to us that staff have the opportunity to develop themselves in their roles.*

Turnbull brought in Train to Gain to carry out a free skills assessment, looking at staff skills and the zoo's goals for the coming year. Together, she and her skills broker drew up a training plan to help zoo staff meet the new challenges.

Eight staff members signed up to do NVQs in customer service in order to improve their communication, time management and personal organisation skills. Six more chose to study other subjects: team leading, business administration and retail. Turnbull concludes:

> *The programme was very flexible, so the learner could progress at a speed that suited them. The training left London Zoo staff better equipped to welcome its many visitors, and laid the foundation for an efficient, successful operation.*

...a broker will put you in touch with training providers and source available funding.

72. Find yourself a mentor

Avoid becoming so caught up with providing training for your employees that you forget your own training and development. No matter how senior or experienced you are, you can still learn and improve. Many senior executives find that mentoring is an excellent way of doing this.

Working with a mentor simply involves meeting once a month, or once a quarter, with a more experienced individual who understands your sector but can provide an impartial point of view. The mentor listens to the challenges you are facing, and offers advice and support.

If you can find someone suitable they probably will be very complimented to be asked, and might perhaps offer their advice without charge.

73. Take advantage of cheap courses at local colleges

If you need to develop skills in specialised areas such as legacy marketing, managing volunteers, charity taxation and so on, you are likely to need to use a training provider that specialises in the voluntary sector. However, for more generalised skills, such as direct mail campaigns, people management and basic bookkeeping, begin by looking at what courses your local colleges have on offer. These may be subsidised, so a great deal cheaper.

Your local college may be able to structure its courses around your needs.

Further and higher education institutions increasingly are keen to sell their courses to organisations such as yours. Your local college will be pleased to hear from you, and may be able to structure its courses around your needs. This can be an excellent way of securing flexible, high-quality teaching at very reasonable rates.

74. Join your local group training association

Group training associations are training and development centres that are owned and shared by local employers. The scheme has been run as a not-for-profit organisation since the 1960s. It covers most sectors, and is a way of pooling resources and providing low-cost training at cost price. (See: www.grouptraining associations.org.uk.)

75. Don't forget to train your volunteers

You need to take volunteer training just as seriously as you take staff training. Without proper training, volunteers can incur you a whole raft of costs. Know what skills and knowledge are needed for each volunteer role, put a system in place for assessing existing competencies, and then seek good-quality training to address any gaps. No matter how pressing the need, do not allow volunteers to do any work on behalf of your charity until they are fully trained.

Without proper training, volunteers can incur you a whole raft of costs.

76. Book volunteer training through the Institute for Advanced Volunteer Management

Run by the CSV, the Institute for Advanced Volunteer Management offers low-cost training for staff responsible for managing volunteers. This includes an annual three-day residential course. All those delivering the training are volunteers, so prices are extremely competitive. (See: www.csv.org.)

77. Learn from your volunteers

Your volunteers will need training in the specific tasks that they perform for you, but don't forget that they will have a wealth of skills and knowledge already on which you could draw. Send out a questionnaire asking them to list their specialist skills, or circulate a list of your organisation's training needs and ask if anyone has skills in these areas. There are few people who do not enjoy sharing their expertise with an interested audience, so many of your volunteers might be only too happy to help in this way.

There are few people who do not enjoy sharing their expertise with an interested audience...

78. Encourage your staff to volunteer

An excellent way to grow the skills and experience of your staff is to encourage them to take on activities outside of work which train volunteers in key skills that employers always need, such as problem-solving, people management, planning, organisation and communication. Why pay for your staff to develop those skills when they can learn them elsewhere at no cost to you? Organisations spend thousands of pounds training volunteers for roles such as becoming a Special Constable, organising a sports team or joining the Reserve Forces or the Territorial Army. You could even look at other charities, such as the British Red Cross, which offer comprehensive training and experience for volunteers in certain areas.

Why pay for your staff to develop skills when they can learn them elsewhere?

79. Run staff training at other internal events

A major cost of training is getting everyone together in one place, so try to run courses when everyone is already in the same place. Could you take a morning out of your annual conference to train everyone involved in your charity about a broad topic? Or could you take 20 minutes at a weekly management meeting to cover a more specific topic? Do this often enough and not only will you reduce your training expenditure, you also will embed training deeply within the culture of your organisation.

80. Use online conferencing

Online conferencing allows you to bring people together for a training session without the need for travel, accommodation and refreshments. This technology now offers much more than a phone conversation between more than two people. You can use webcams to see who is speaking. You can all look at the same documents online, seeing other participants writing or drawing on them. You can have your calls recorded and the minutes emailed to you.

Online conferencing offers much more than a phone conversation between more than two people.

In recent years costs have tumbled, and reliability has come on in leaps and bounds. Take a look at providers such as WebEx (www.webex.co.uk), PoWowNow (www.powwownow.co.uk) and WiredRed (www.wired red.co.uk), and see how much you could save.

81. Cross-train your employees

Many employees will call in sick at some point, or will have to take time off to deal with crises at home. This might leave you needing to bring in temporary cover for them, and this will be expensive. A cheaper option is to cross-train your employees so that they can step into their colleagues' shoes.

...get everyone to buddy someone in a similar role.

Begin by getting everyone to 'buddy' someone in a similar role. Set up times when they will show each other how they do their jobs, and then arrange shadowing sessions. Their new skills should be sufficient to allow them to keep things ticking over for a day or two. If you want to take it a step further, arrange specific skills and knowledge training to ensure that you need never pay for temporary cover again.

82. Buy in books instead of training

You are reading this, so you don't need to be persuaded of the value of books as a source of information, but how often do your colleagues read books related to their jobs? Rather than spending £150 on a training course for one person on one subject, why not buy the the latest books instead? Distribute them around your staff, and have a weekly lunch meeting where everyone brings one good idea from the book that they are reading to discuss with the group. Then, whenever a member of your team needs to learn about a topic, give them the book to read before rushing to send them on a training course.

83. Evaluate all your training

Avoid wasting money on any training that is not producing a directly measurable improvement in performance. All too often, training providers simply ask delegates at the end of a course what they thought of the course. The delegates have spent several hours with that person and probably are enthused by what they have learned. Consequently, these 'happy sheets' are notorious for producing artificially positive feedback.

... set up systems to measure improvements in performance over time.

Instead, set up systems to measure improvements in performance over time. Whether or not your staff enjoyed a training session is irrelevant, except in terms of motivating those staff. Before you send them on the course, identify the specific outcome that you expect, know how you will measure it, then perform that evaluation. If a course fails to achieve the desired outcome, stop spending money on it.

Chapter 6

Culture

84. Build a culture of cost saving

Of course, your staff are more than a cost – they are your greatest asset. If you are to make long-term cost savings in your organisation, you need them. You might be convinced of the need to cut costs. You might be brimming with great ideas for how to make these savings. However, unless you can get your staff on board, you will struggle to bring these plans to fruition. After all, it is those employees who make the everyday decisions about purchasing cheaper services, recycling paper, reducing water use, reusing materials and so on.

However, it can be difficult to get those members of staff engaged with the idea. They may see it as yet another initiative from management, or as something which has little to do with their jobs. Or they might be full of enthusiasm, but when it comes to it, the pressure of getting the job done results in cost-saving considerations taking a backseat.

Your first step towards building a culture of cost-consciousness in your charity is to lead from the top. You will have almost no chance of getting staff to buy into your economising drive unless they are convinced of the need to do it, and see it as a central to their work at the charity. So, you need to build a culture of cost saving.

. . . your staff are more than a cost – they are your greatest asset.

85. Make it clear that you are cutting costs, not corners

Make it crystal clear that in no shape or form are you cutting corners in your core mission.

The first step towards building a cost-saving culture is to reassure staff publicly. Some people, when they hear the phrase 'cutting costs', automatically think of 'cutting corners'. You need to halt this thinking right at the outset. Make it crystal clear that in no shape or form are you cutting corners in your core mission. Whether your charity provides services, seeks to shift public opinion, carries out research or has some other charitable purpose, you aim must be to continue to deliver that as well as you can, within the budget at your disposal.

In fact, a key motivation for your cost-cutting drive is to increase the amount of money you have for this work, to demonstrate that you are not cutting corners in this area – or in fact in any area of your work. Make sure that everyone is clear about this so that no one sees your changes as an opportunity to slack off, or resists your changes because they think that it will damage the charity's work.

86. Make cost-cutting everyone's problem

…get as many people as possible involved in generating and implementing ideas.

Many organisations decide to appoint a cost-cutting champion. This does ensure that someone has ownership of the issue, but it can lead other members to staff to think of it as 'someone else's problem'. It is far better to get as many people as possible involved in generating and implementing ideas.

87. Set cost-cutting targets

Rather than announcing vague intentions to cut costs, give people a target for which to aim. State that you are going to cut costs by a certain percentage. Make the target achievable but challenging. Set an annual target, and break this down into monthly goals. Remember that the idea may make many people feel threatened, so make it clear how these cuts will benefit them as individuals and the organisation as a whole.

88. Make your figures meaningful

Cost-cutting lends itself to figures. For example, you might explain to your staff how you have cut your travel budget by 7 per cent in three months, or how you are spending 3 per cent less on IT maintenance. However, while these might sound impressive, for many of your staff they will just be numbers. So instead, try to relate the figure to something more tangible. For example, show them that cutting postage costs by 5 per cent means that you can shelter a dozen more animals.

89. Give staff an incentive to cut costs

Try offering a monthly prize to the member of staff who carries out the most innovative and effective cost-cutting activity. The prize doesn't need to be expensive – perhaps a bunch of flowers, or dinner for two at a local restaurant. More important is the recognition that accompanies it. Make sure that your chief executive awards the prize in front of the rest of the company. The individual who receives the award will feel good about themselves, and everyone else will want to win it next time round.

Try offering a monthly prize...

90. Ask staff for cost-saving ideas

This book is packed full of tips to help you cut costs in your charity. It should spark dozens more ideas of your own. However, remember that your staff will have great ideas too. Using their ideas is not just good because it

...people tend to be much more enthusiastic when implementing their own ideas.

draws on a potentially rich source of innovation, but people tend to be much more enthusiastic when implementing their own ideas. So, ask your staff for their ideas. Offer a prize to whoever comes up with the best idea each month.

91. Set up a cost-saving ideas box

Once you have told your staff that you want to hear their ideas, you need to create opportunities for them to share those ideas. Hold meetings, and ask everyone to bring an idea for saving money. Set up an email address where people can email their ideas. Buy an actual box, label it 'Cost-saving ideas', and place it in the middle of the office. Look at it once a week or once a month, and see what people have come up with – within a year you are bound to have generated at least a dozen excellent new ideas.

Hold meetings, and ask everyone to bring an idea for saving money.

92. Acknowledge contributions

When your staff come up with cost-saving ideas, it is important that you acknowledge their contribution. You don't have to implement every idea that they have, but you do have to let them know that you have noticed their effort, you appreciate it, and you have given their suggestions due consideration. This acknowledgement could consist of a quiet word in passing in the corridor, or it could be a public announcement – but however you do it, make sure it gets done.

93. Get into the details

When one of your department heads comes to you and explains that there are no more areas where they can cut costs, you might be tempted to believe them. Indeed, it might well be the case. However, before you do accept this and turn your attention elsewhere, take the time to sit down with them and go through everything that their department does. Look at it day-by-day, task-by-task, person-by-person. You might be surprised by how much potential for cost-cutting you uncover. Very often you will find that once you have opened up someone's mind to the possibilities, they will become one of your most ardent and enthusiastic cost-cutters.

94. Recognise the power of collective thinking

When a group of people comes together to overcome a shared obstacle, very often they can become much more than the sum of their parts. Next time you are facing a thorny issue and are about to hire an expensive consultant, try asking your team for a solution. You might be surprised by their ideas.

95. Continually educate staff on cost-cutting

It is not enough for your staff to want to help you cut costs – they must know *how* to do so. Identify development needs for groups and individuals, and then provide the training and individual coaching that they need.

Take every possible opportunity to reinforce the cost-cutting message. Use team meetings, noticeboards, email, the intranet, the staff newsletter and every other possible medium to remind people of the importance of cost-cutting, and to show how the organisation is performing against its monthly and annual targets.

... often once you've opened up someone's mind to the possibilities, they will become one of your most ardent cost-cutters.

Take every possible opportunity to reinforce the cost-cutting message.

96. Stop making so many mistakes

...UK businesses are spending 40 billion hours a year on correcting errors in the workplace...

Recognise that while new ideas for cutting costs are important, vast sums of money are lost every day by organisations that do not do the basics as well as they could. According to a recent survey commissioned by the British Quality Foundation (BQF) and the Chartered Quality Institute, UK businesses are spending 40 billion hours a year on correcting errors in the workplace, at a total cost of £79.6 billion to the UK economy.

The survey of 2,500 UK employees found that 53 per cent of UK workers are wasting up to 10 per cent of their time on correcting mistakes, only 15 per cent of employees believe that their organisations deliver on time every time, and 38 per cent of employees say that their organisations do not measure the cost of mistakes.

The BQF argues that by putting in place recognised quality systems, every organisation can perform significantly better in all areas – including error levels, customer service, internal communications, risk management and waste reduction. So apply this principle to your organisation. Encourage staff to look at their work, to identify the mistakes they repeatedly make, and to take action to ensure that they stop making them.

(For advice on how to develop and implement those systems, see the BQF website: www.quality-foundation. co.uk.)

Chapter 7

Purchasing

97. Set budgets

While people are probably your most significant single cost, they are far from the only one. Your charity buys all sorts of items every day. It can be tempting to see cost-cutting as a process of reducing the number of items that you buy. However, there are ways of buying the same number of items but paying less for them. The key thing is to put in place an effective purchasing system, and the first step towards doing that is to set accurate budgets.

A remarkable number of charities operate without budgets. If yours is one of them, stop reading now and start allocating budgets for your expenditure. If you don't know how much you have available to spend, and how much you are actually spending, you can never hope to make an informed decision on any individual purchase. Buying blind without a budget is an almost certain way to waste money, to spend more than you have, and to cause financial problems for your charity.

... there are ways of buying the same number of items but paying less for them.

98. Know what you are spending

Knowledge is power, and this is never more true than when it comes to controlling your organisation's spending. You need to have complete, accurate and up-to-date information on all of your organisation's expenditure.

However, achieving this can be more difficult than it sounds. Individual departments can be protective about the precise details of their expenditure. Scratch beneath

...develop a clear and straightforward system through which individual departments report their spending.

the surface, and you might find that they are less than certain about what they spend.

The answer is to develop a clear and straightforward system through which individual departments report their spending. You don't want it to take up too much of their time, so make it as simple as possible, but make sure that it gives you all the information you need. If your staff still fail to give you the information you want, replace them with people who will.

99. Look ahead, not backwards

It can be tempting when devising a budget to look simply at what was spent last year and to use that, plus a little extra for inflation, as next year's budget. However, it is far better to spend some time assessing exactly what will be needed next year. This forward-looking approach ensures that you will spend only what is necessary, rather than using up budget just because it is there.

...spend some time assessing exactly what will be needed next year.

100. Get into details on budgets

The more detail you can get into on your budgets, the better. If you can predict exactly what you will have to spend and when, and exactly what funds you will have coming in, you can make much more informed decisions about discretionary spending. Also, you will be much more accurate, and can avoid any unpleasant surprises. Of course, this need for detail must be balanced with the time it takes. Budgeting matters, but do not let it take over your life!

101. Know the full cost before buying

Often, it can be tempting to jump at a price that looks low. However, it is always better to take time to think about the full cost before signing on the dotted line. Find out what extra costs there will be. Think about the running costs, service costs, delivery and optional extras. Are taxes included in the price quoted? How much will finance cost? How about the cost of disposal? When you add in all these factors, what seems like a low headline price can turn out to be very expensive. Find out the truth before committing yourself.

102. Ask for donations before you buy

Before you buy an item, ask whether the company in question will donate it to you. You have a unique point of difference as a charity: you might not have the budgets of commercial organisations, but you do enjoy the goodwill of many people. Use it, and you will find that not only can you reduce many of your costs, you might be able to eliminate some altogether.

103. Ask for a pre-payment discount

According to conventional accounting theory, it is always far better to keep hold of cash and spread payments over time. This is indeed wise advice. It is far better to have money earning interest in your account than in your supplier's account. It is also better to keep hold of your money until you are certain that you need the product or service.

... you may be able to negotiate a discount for payment in advance.

However, because your suppliers are following this rule too, you may be able to negotiate a discount from them for payment in advance. You even may be able to agree a discount that is worth more than the interest that you would earn from having the money in the bank. If that is the case, and you are certain that you will use the products, then paying in advance makes a great deal of sense.

104. Ask for charity discounts

Many companies will have a charity price.

Even if you are unable to negotiate a donation, try asking for a charity discount. Most charities already do this, so if you are not asking for one, you are missing a major opportunity to save money. Many companies will have a charity price. Some service providers, such as marketing agencies, will even offer to work for free. They see these *pro bono* relationships as their chance to give something back to society. It also does their public image no harm.

So, make sure you take full advantage. Spend a few hours contacting all your suppliers and asking them if they can give you a better price because you are a charity. If they refuse, look around to see if one of their competitors will. It might take a bit of time, but you will be surprised by how much you can save.

105. Buy in bulk – but with care

Bulk purchases are not always the best bet.

Whenever you purchase a product or service for your charity, think about whether you could buy more and negotiate a discount for buying in bulk. Bear in mind, though, that the calculation can be complex. Bulk purchases are not always the best bet.

For example, will you use enough of the item in question to make it worthwhile buying a year's supply now, or will you be looking at a pile of unused stock this time next year? Even if you do use all the items, what will it cost to store them?

It is a difficult balance to get right. Often, the only way to estimate future consumption levels is to know about past consumption. So, in all but the most exceptional cases, you should never buy in bulk on the first order. Once you are sure that you will be using an item in sufficiently high volumes, then you can start making the savings.

106. Negotiate an annual deal

Just as it can make sense to pay for products or services in advance – if you are sure that you need them, and you can agree a large enough discount – it can make sense to arrange an annual deal with your regular service providers.

If you give them the security of an annual contract rather than a series of one-off jobs, they will be able to invest in the people, technology and systems that will not only improve their service to you, but also should allow them to make a better margin on their work for you.

Make sure that they share this enhanced profit with you in the form of a reduced price but be careful not to hammer their price down so low that they are simply tied into an undesirable long-term contract with you. The relationship needs to be mutually beneficial.

...it can make sense to arrange an annual deal with your regular service providers.

107. Buy at the right time of year

We all know that beachwear is cheapest in September and that the best month to buy Christmas cards is January, but have you thought about how you can apply this principle to your business purchasing? Look at everything you buy and see if you could get it more cheaply by buying it at a certain time of year.

108. Negotiate good credit terms with your suppliers

The longer your suppliers give you to pay their bills, the better for your cashflow, and the more interest you can earn on money in the bank. The best time to negotiate good terms is at the start of a relationship, but you can do it later on if necessary.

The best time to negotiate good terms is at the start of a relationship...

Go through your current supplier relationships. Do you pay any in advance where this is not the industry norm? Could you shift any seven-day payment terms to 28 days?

Once you have identified a few targets, give them a call with your proposal. You will not get far if you simply call asking if you can keep hold of their money for longer: be prepared to offer something in return. The secret to good negotiation is to give the other person something that is important to them but has little value to you. Would it help them to aggregate deliveries? Could you use their premises when they are otherwise unoccupied?

Think laterally about what you can offer. You may be surprised at what good deals you can strike.

109. Never accept the first offer

Andrew Lees, a consultant at cost-cutting firm Expense Reduction Analysts, has worked with charities such as the British Lung Foundation and the Royal British Legion, helping them to cut costs. He offers the following advice on how to drive prices down:

*Never accept
the first offer.*

> Never accept the first offer. Business is tough at the moment, and suppliers – no matter which market they operate in – will be keen to get your business. So it never does any harm to go back to them with a lower offer.

110. Don't buy business products

Very often, business products are more expensive than similar products aimed at consumers. For example, look at bank accounts and mobile phone tariffs. Both charge business customers more than they charge consumers. While this extra cost usually ensures higher levels of service, continuity of service guarantees and so on, think carefully about whether these extras are worth the higher cost. If they are not, simply buy the consumer version instead.

111. Don't buy from resellers

Buy anything from resellers – whether it is software, furniture or anything else – and you are overpaying already, as they will add a percentage on to the price that they pay for the product or service. By going direct to the manufacturer or provider, you can cut your costs by exactly the same percentage.

This is not to say that resellers have no value. Often when you are buying something for the first time, the advice and expertise of a third party can be invaluable. However, once you know what you need, you are better off simply getting it at the cheapest price possible.

By going direct to the manufacturer or provider, you can cut your costs...

112. Buy online

Before you buy something, check to see whether you can get it cheaper online. Very often, because websites do not have to pay for retail space or large numbers of staff, they can offer significant savings. Get into the habit of checking online before handing over the cash, and you will save money in the long run.

Get into the habit of checking online before handing over the cash...

113. Use online auctions

The Office of Government Commerce recently reported that it had saved 50 per cent on the cost of 5,000 laptops and 20 per cent on the cost of 5,000 PCs. It had achieved this through online reverse auctions. These auctions work by forcing suppliers to bid decreasing prices for the contract offered, in response to competitors' bids. Only the buyer can see who is offering each price.

There is no reason why you cannot achieve similar cost savings on a wide range of services and products. A quick online search will reveal several sites on which you can

61

host your reverse auction. The cost is small compared to the potential savings.

Bear in mind that price should not be the sole purchasing criterion for many goods. Suppliers hate these auctions, so this is not the way to build positive, long-term relationships with them. However, for commodity purchases it can be an extremely effective method of saving large sums of money.

114. Run pilots before signing on the dotted line

Never agree to any major expenditure without first running a pilot. If the item in question is new software, ask one or two members of staff to use it for a month before committing. If it is a major direct mail campaign, try it out on a small sample before giving the printers the green light. Whatever it is, avoid committing yourself until you are certain that it will work.

...avoid committing yourself until you are certain that it will work.

115. Get what you are entitled to

Often, suppliers justify expensive service contracts by including extras such as free servicing or insurance. They include them because they are confident that few of their customers will ever notice they are in there, much less take advantage of them. Don't let them get away with it. Go through your service contracts and take up every free offer itemised – you have paid for it, so get what you are entitled to. If you check carefully, you might even find that you are paying for something twice.

116. Set up a local benchmarking group

How do you know if you are paying a fair price for the products and services that your organisation uses? One way of being sure is to set up a benchmarking group with similar organisations in your area. Meet once a month to discuss what you have paid, or you could even set up a simple website where members can log their purchases. This will help you to ensure that no one pays too much.

...set up a benchmarking group with similar organisations in your area.

117. Form a consortium to buy expensive items

No doubt you have a fairly lengthy list of major items that you would like to buy for your charity, but every year there is not enough left in the budget to make it possible. If you are like most charities, the list probably gets longer every year, and gradually the items shift from the 'desirable' column to the 'necessary' one.

Take a look at that list now, and think about whether you could make any of those items affordable by sharing the cost with another organisation. If the item is specific to charity work – say a minibus to transport service users – you almost certainly will find another charity in your area that also needs one and which might be willing to split the cost.

You can even look beyond the voluntary sector. Think about what you could share with local businesses, or with schools and hospitals. Remember: the more organisations who join your consortium, the lower the costs for everyone.

Think about what you could share with local businesses, or with schools and hospitals.

118. Consider payroll sharing

If you have a small number of staff, administering the payroll will be very expensive for you. You have to pay someone to keep the records, to ensure payments are made on time, to calculate correct tax deductions and so on. You also will need to pay for software to store these records.

...reduce costs by sharing them with other, similar organisations.

You can reduce these costs by sharing them with other, similar organisations. Simply identify the organisations that you think might be facing the same issue as you, and call them up to suggest the idea. The worst they can do is to say no. If they say yes, you will have found a great way of reducing the cost of the person doing the work and the software that they need to do it.

119. Simplify your purchase order system

If you are raising a purchase order for every single purchase, you are wasting resources. You might even find that you are spending more on the purchasing process than you are on the goods themselves. Streamline the system so that you issue the fewest number of purchase orders that allow you to keep control of what you are buying.

120. Check all your invoices

Invoice fraud is a growing crime. It is remarkably simple, and worryingly effective. The fraudsters send invoices to organisations and wait for the cheques to roll in. They succeed because a remarkable number of organisations fail to check their invoices – they just pay them.

...set up a system to ensure that someone is checking every invoice you pay.

In the same way, you might be overpaying legitimate suppliers who have made honest mistakes on their invoices to you. It happens, and it is up to you to spot these mistakes. So, set up a system to ensure that someone is checking every invoice you pay. Make sure that the goods were provided, the amount is correct, and that you only pay once.

121. Pay suppliers on time

There is a school of thought in business which advocates paying suppliers late. Certainly, this can do wonders for the short-term balance sheet. However, it does very little for the long-term reputation and performance of your organisation.

Start paying your suppliers late, and before long you will reap the consequences. They will spend less time on your account. They will cease to provide goods and services that meet basic standards. They will see you as a customer rather than a business partner.

Start paying your suppliers late, and before long you will reap the consequences.

You might think that this does not matter because you can simply go to one of their competitors. Initially, you will be able to do this. However, the problem soon will repeat itself there. Before long you will get a reputation and, while people will want to supply you, they will do it without any enthusiasm or commitment. You will have lost a key part of that indefinable something that marks out successful organisations from average ones.

Paying suppliers late is always a false economy. Don't do it.

Chapter 8

Property

122. Consider renting or buying

For most charities, the largest cost after people is property. There is much you can do to trim this expense.

Begin by looking at whether you would be better off by renting or buying. Whether you rent or buy your properties at the moment, look into the options available to you. Would a commercial mortgage work out less expensive in the long run than your rent payments? Could you release essential capital by selling your properties and renting them back, or by moving to cheaper rented premises?

Could you release essential capital by selling your properties?

123. Ask your landlord to donate part of your rent

If you rent your premises, have you tried asking your landlord if they would like to make a donation to charity in the form of a rent reduction? It is not as cheeky as it sounds. If you rent from an individual, they may welcome the opportunity to give something back to society. Meanwhile, a growing number of companies are keen to be socially responsible. Your suggestion could be just the opportunity they are looking for – at worst, they can only say no.

124. Negotiate a discount on your rent

Unless you are fortunate enough to have charitable landlords, you have to find a more creative way of persuading them to accept a lower rent. If you rent, this is a major item in your outgoings column, so it is worth spending some time on. If you can cut this cost by just a few percentage points, you will save a lot of money for your charity.

So, how do you persuade your landlords to accept less rent from you? Just going and asking is unlikely to work. It might do, if the local rental market is falling and they know that they will struggle to get tenants paying as much as you. Assemble your evidence: find out what your neighbours are paying, and use this to show that tenants in comparable space are paying rents that are 5 per cent lower than yours. Then offer to accept a reduction of only 4 per cent. Get it right, and they will be only too ready to accept.

However, if you are not in a falling rental market you still might be able to give your landlords a good reason to accept lower rent from you. The key is to think of something you can give them that they value. Would they accept 95 per cent of the current money if it was paid quarterly in advance rather than monthly? Could you offer to do their post or banking at the same time as you do yours? Do you always have unused stock that you could give to them?

Every landlord is different, and the only way you will find out what yours need is by talking to them. So, go and have a chat or pick up the phone. You might be surprised by what you find out.

. . . give your landlords a good reason to accept lower rent from you.

125. Sublet unused space

If you are unable to persuade your landlord to reduce your rent, or if you are your own landlord, you will need to look at ways to use the space that you do have more effectively. If you have any space sitting unused, let it out. It might be office, storage, parking or any other type of space. If you own it – or worse, if you are paying for it – you are wasting money if you allow it to sit empty.

If you own it you are wasting money if you allow it to sit empty.

126. Minimise excess stock

If you are holding unsold stock, you are not only losing out on the potential sale, but you are also paying for warehouse space. Try to plan to reduce this problem as far as possible by using the stock up, and ordering less. You may reach a point where it is cheaper for you to sell the stock at less than you paid for it than it is to keep storing it. Don't shy away from this decision. Cut your losses, put your hand up to your error, and ensure that you don't make it again.

127. Use cheap storage

Every organisation has to keep financial information for several years. You may need to keep other information, such as beneficiary, donor and employee records. Before long all these files can start to take up space, and it is rarely cost-efficient to rent office space for storing folders. Using specialist storage space is much cheaper, and clearing out these old records can feel like an invigorating spring clean.

...it is rarely cost-efficient to rent office space for storing folders.

128. Share space with another charity

It is almost certain that you are not the only charity in your area that struggles to make the finances add up.

Doing this is the number one challenge for almost everyone who has the tough job of running a charity. Right now, there is probably another charity manager a few streets away who is worrying about how they will pay the rent on head office, whether they can afford to provide that service to beneficiaries next year, or whether that satellite operation is still financially feasible.

Very often these problems are caused by over-supply of facilities combined with fluctuations in demand and funding. You don't want to move to a smaller head office because next year you expect to be awarded increased funding, and so will need to recruit again. You don't want to cut that service or close that satellite office, because you expect demand for your services to grow in those areas over the next decade.

So, why not work with that other charity to share your costs in the short term? Why not move into the same office, or deliver your services from the same location? This does not need to be a full merger – just a temporary measure to reduce costs until one or both organisations can afford to cover them in full again.

...there is probably another charity manager a few streets away worrying about how they will pay the rent...

129. Sell car-parking space

If you have a car park with your premises, you are very lucky. It is a great perk you can offer to your staff, and you probably find it much easier to use the handy staff car park than to have to park a few streets away or to make do with public transport.

However, you are also wasting a huge amount of money. By selling or leasing the land you could free up hundreds of thousands of pounds, or possibly millions – making it useful capital that could generate income for the organisation.

At the same time, you will be encouraging your staff to get a little bit of invigorating exercise by having to park a little further away. Or you all will have to get public transport to work, and so reduce your harmful environmental impact.

130. Encourage remote working

The advent of the Internet and affordable mobile and fixed-line telephony has made remote working more feasible than ever before. In fact, it is more than feasible – for many office-based employees and employers, it is positively desirable.

...for many office-based employees and employers, remote working is positively desirable.

For you, it can offer a wider pool of talent from which to recruit – you no longer need to limit your searches to people who can spend eight hours a day wherever your office happens to be located. Also, it can save you money. The less time your staff spend in the office, the less you have to spend on office space, furniture, refreshments, and so on.

For employees, it frees them from the drudgery of the daily commute. It allows them to spend more time with their family or on their hobbies outside of work. If it goes well, you will have happier and healthier members of staff who approach their work positively and enthusiastically. You might even find that without the daily commute they spend more time on their actual work.

Perhaps you doubt that it will work out this way. You might worry that if you are not there to keep an eye on what they are doing, they will slack off. This might well be the case. If it is, don't give up on the idea of remote working, but look closely into your recruitment and management. Are you really hiring the right people? Are you motivating them properly?

If your staff need you breathing down their neck day in, day out, then something has gone wrong somewhere. Root out this more fundamental problem, and once it is resolved you can take advantage of the cost savings and broader benefits of remote working.

131. Introduce hotdesking

Talk a walk around your offices and count how many desks are unoccupied. Is it 10 per cent, 20 per cent or more? With people out at meetings, spending the afternoon in your own internal meeting rooms, on holiday, off sick, or working from home, it is unlikely that every desk is always full.

This means that you are constantly paying for desks to be empty. As a result, your premises are bigger than they need to be. You are paying for furniture, computers, phones and other equipment that is sitting unoccupied and idle. How much money are you wasting in this way?

By introducing hotdesking you could reduce this waste significantly. Hotdesking is a way of working in which no one has their own desk. When people are in the office, they find an available workstation and log in to their own personalised desktop. It means that you can reduce the number of workstations that you pay for, and so save money.

Bear in mind that some people will feel threatened by this. People like to have their own space – their own territory where they feel comfortable and safe. They will complain that they cannot find vital documents and will worry that there might not be a desk free for them to use.

Be prepared for these objections. Some of them will be genuine – for example, you might need to give everyone central storage space for their documents and equipment. Others will be less so, but this does not mean you should ignore them. Explain why you are making this change, make the case for it, and show them how it will free up vital funds to be used elsewhere.

... hotdesking will free up vital funds to be used elsewhere.

132. Move to smaller premises

Even if you cannot cut the cost of the space that you own or rent, and you cannot use the space that you do have more productively, there are still options open to you. The most obvious is to move to smaller premises.

You will not be alone in doing this. The *UK Cities Monitor 2008*, published by estate agent Cushman and Wakefield, found that a quarter of companies expected to reduce space requirements in order to cut costs. One-fifth intended to consolidate staff into one building.

Indeed, recent research from corporate property firm CoreNet revealed that many organisations give their employees much more space than they actually need. It found that employees tend to have an average of 100 sq ft each. Some experts believe it is possible to halve that space without any impact on productivity.

...look into how you could cope with a smaller space.

So, work out how much space each of your employees takes up. If it is more than 100 sq ft, you almost certainly can save money by moving to a smaller office. If it is between 50 and 100 sq ft, look into how you could cope with a smaller space. Be careful, though, that your staff do not feel cramped, as this could become a false economy in the long run.

133. Move into serviced offices

Many smaller charities may find it more cost-effective to pay for a serviced office than to retain a full-time administrator. In serviced offices, a central team of administrators provides telephone answering, post and other secretarial services for a set monthly fee. Be careful not to leave yourself under-resourced, but there is no harm in exploring this as an option.

134. Move into a new development

In the first few years of the 21st century, property developers invested huge sums of money in building serviced office space. They were encouraged by the availability of cheap finance and the expectation that the economy would continue to grow and, with it, demand for serviced office space. Hower, they have been sorely disappointed. The 2008 financial collapse meant that acres of this space now lie empty.

This is bad news for property developers and the companies which now own these developments, but it could be excellent news for you. Take a hour today to ring round a few local developments and see what sort of deal they can offer you. Many of them are so desperate for tenants that they will offer extraordinarily good deals.

... ring round a few local developments and see what sort of deal they can offer you.

135. Relocate to a cheaper part of the country

Do you really need to be located in a city centre? How much would you save on rent if you moved to a business park near the ring road? For that matter, could you save by relocating to another part of the country altogether? Your transfer does not have to be as dramatic as moving from Kensington to north Wales – even within one county there can be dramatic differences in the cost of property.

... could you save by relocating to another part of the country?

It is not just property costs that you could cut by relocating, you might find that suppliers in the new area will quote you lower prices. Get the location right, and you could cut your travel costs too. Perhaps most significantly, you might be able to reduce your wage bill by siting yourself in an area with a lower cost of living. The move itself will be expensive and disruptive, but it could pay off in the long term.

136. Use a property search agency

In 2006, the Children's Heart Foundation needed new office space. It hired a property search agency called the Charity Supply Company to search for the property. The agency came up with four different offices to choose from, each of which had a better specification and a lower price than it was expecting. In the end, it chose one that resulted in a saving of £15,000 a year.

The Charity Supply Company claims that in eight years it has taken on 25 office relocations for charities, saving them a total of more than £1 million. Unlike most surveyors or estate agents, it works exclusively for charities needing new offices, and is paid only if it saves money for the charity.

The company says this means it searches harder to find the right property, and negotiates harder with landlords and other agents to get it at the right price. It adds that its clients save an average of 35 per cent of their budgets, and that it has never failed to match the brief and beat the budget.

... investigate the services of a property search agency before you sign your next lease...

Given these impressive statistics, it could be well worth investigating the services of a property search agency before you sign your next lease or buy your next commercial property. The Charity Supply Company (www.charitysupply.co.uk) is only one agency – a simple Google search will produce many more, all of which will be willing to help you.

137. Minimise dilapidations costs

Dilapidations costs are what you have to pay at the end of a lease for repairs and internal decoration. Provision for this is usually written into a lease, but many commercial tenants tend to ignore these clauses, seeing them as insignificant compared to the cost of the rent. They are wrong. These costs can be high, so it is important to take steps to minimise them.

Aside from keeping the building in good repair and decorative order, the most important step that you can take is to have the building checked over by a building surveyor, or at the very least an experienced builder, before you sign the lease. They should identify any pre-existing defects, which should be recorded on the lease in the form of a 'schedule of condition', ideally with full photographic evidence.

... have the building checked over by a building surveyor...

138. Don't use removal firms

When you move office, don't spend thousands of pounds on a removal firm. Simply instruct every employee to pack up the files, books, computers, stationery, phones, furniture and so on around them, and have them all spend a day loading and unloading it. Everyone does it when they move home, so why not when they move office? It will be a fun day, build a team spirit, and engender a greater sense of ownership of the new office. Plus it will save a lot of money.

Chapter 9

Office services

139. Share property management services

When you have a reasonably-sized property portfolio, it is not just the property itself that is expensive. You also need to employ an army of estate surveyors, building surveyors, facilities staff and property helpdesk operators.

Early in 2009 Charles Nall, corporate services director at The Children's Society, raised the idea of a joint venture between charities with large or dispersed networks of offices or project buildings, in order to enable them to share these property management services. He argued that using property management services through a joint venture would be 20 to 50 per cent cheaper than using a medium-sized surveying firm.

Take a look into what schemes like this are available. If you do not find any, look into setting one up yourself. Identify any charities you know which are facing bills as large as yours for these services, and simply ask them if they would be interested.

140. Do basic painting and decorating yourself

Why waste money on painters and decorators?

Why waste money on painters and decorators? Just get half a dozen of your staff to stay behind one evening and spend a couple of hours doing the job. Buy them all some pizza and a few drinks to thank them for it. You might find that, as well as saving your organisation a few pounds, those who do it enjoy themselves and get to know each other a bit better.

There may be more basic odd jobs you can do yourself, but before you go ahead make sure you consider the health and safety implications (see tip 321).

141. Cut cleaning costs

Do you really need someone coming in every day for a few hours to clean your premises? How long does it take for bins to fill up, or for floors and surfaces to become dirty? The chances are that you probably don't know because you have never actually seen them full or dirty. While no one wants to work in squalor, you probably don't need to spend quite as much on cleaning services as you currently do. Try reducing them by 20 per cent and see if anyone notices the difference.

Try reducing your cleaning services by 20 per cent and see if anyone notices.

142. Cut down on external catering

When you have a meeting that runs over lunch, you are unlikely to think about going out to an expensive restaurant. After all, you are a charity executive, not an over-indulged city slicker. By popping down to the local café and asking them to prepare a plate of sandwiches for your lunch meeting or by picking up a boxed sandwich platter from your nearest supermarket you are certainly going some way to save your charity money.

143. Ban the use of couriers

How much does your organisation spend on couriers every year? It is very easy to let this expenditure spiral out of control without really feeling like you are spending much on it. After all, if a courier is always a last-minute option, where is the incentive to plan ahead and send an item the day before by normal mail?

. . . ban the use of couriers in your organisation.

The simplest and most effective solution is to ban the use of couriers in your organisation. If your colleagues know that they no longer have the safety net of a courier, they will make sure that they have the package ready to post the day before.

Of course, in absolute emergencies it might still be necessary to use couriers – but issuing a firm rule such as this sends a clear message, and will go a long way to cutting unnecessary spending.

144. Pay less for your waste disposal

Waste disposal is expensive. With rising costs and decreasing availability of space, the cost of landfill has soared in the past five years. This, combined with rising transportation costs, means that for many organisations waste disposal has grown from an irritating miscellaneous item on the balance sheet into a significant cost. It goes without saying that the best way of reducing this expense is to reduce the amount of waste that your organisation generates. Educate your staff about the need to reuse materials, and recycle where possible.

Educate your staff about the need to reuse materials, and recycle where possible.

However, there is a limit to how much you can achieve in this way. You also need to look at ways of reducing the actual unit cost of disposing of the waste that you do produce. Make sure you get quotes from all suppliers, as the waste disposal market is changing rapidly, with a large number of new, innovative players entering the market.

Also, bear in mind that one organisation's waste is another person's resource. Just as you might be keen to take a business's redundant office furniture, so a local construction materials supplier might need your old bottles. Time spent researching this and networking among local businesses could turn a cost into an income stream.

145. Encourage the principles of reduce, reuse, recycle

It has long been the mantra of the green movement, but you can use it to reduce your expenditure on office supplies and services: reduce, reuse, recycle. Hold a meeting at which you ask staff to do this. Put up posters around the workplace reminding them.

...reduce, reuse, recycle.

Then, gradually and quietly, reinforce these messages one person at a time. When you see someone needlessly using something, intervene and explain how they could reduce their resource usage. When you see someone throwing away an item which can be reused, talk them through how much you spend on that item, and remind them of what good work your charity could do with those funds. When you see someone not using appropriate recycling bins, let them know what they should be doing.

Not everyone will listen to what you have to say, but some will. In time they will become advocates of reducing, reusing and recycling – and before long they will be advising their colleagues on how to stick to this philosophy. Before you know it, the message will filtered throughout your organisation, and you will be spending a lot less on your supplies and services than you do now.

146. Hold a 'One Bin Day'

For many organisations, the greatest challenge with workplace waste is not that staff are not aware of the issues and the facts, it is translating that awareness into action. You can focus attention on the topic with innovative and fun events such as One Bin Day.

For just one day, remove all bins from your office apart from one.

For just one day, remove all bins from your office apart from one. This will help your staff to see how much waste they produce as a group, and to make them think about what they could use less of, what they could reuse, and what they could recycle.

Chapter 10

Office supplies

147. Monitor office stationery use

Once you have found a cheaper property, or a way to make your existing premises work harder for you, it is time to turn your attention to the cost of running those buildings. An important cost in running any organisation, but one that is often overlooked, is that of office supplies. These tend to be basic items that are ordered once a month or so, with no one paying attention to how many are used or how much each unit costs.

Begin with a look at your stationery. Most offices overspend on stationery: they buy items which are never used, and the items that are used frequently disappear before they wear out or break. While you don't want to start monitoring pen usage or frisking staff to see who is taking staplers home with them, you also don't want to waste money in this area.

Most offices overspend on stationery...

Try to find a sensible middle ground. Tell staff how much you are spending on stationery, show what a 10 per cent saving over a year would allow the charity to do, then work together to achieve that goal. Get this right, and the benefits will go far beyond a 10 per cent cost saving on stationery spending.

148. Downgrade your stationery

Next time you put in a stationery order, go for a slightly cheaper version of everything you normally buy. Having marginally cheaper pens, envelopes, writing pads, document wallets and so on will make very little

81

Having marginally cheaper pens will make very little difference to anyone...

difference to anyone involved with your charity, but it will trim a few pounds off your stationery costs – over a year, that saving will add up.

149. Ask for freebies

Very often, suppliers such as your stationery company will be willing to throw in something for free with every order. You simply have to ask. You might be surprised by what you end up with: it could be a pack of pens, a briefcase, a box of biscuits or a block of photocopier paper – whatever they have to hand that they are willing to throw in to keep you a happy, loyal customer.

150. Cut back on magazines

How many magazines does your organisation subscribe to, and how many are actually read? How many sit unread in reception for a week or a month and end up in the bin? How much does all of this cost your charity?

...there is no sense in paying for something which is never read.

While magazines can be a great source of information, and can provide knowledge which helps your employees to do their jobs more successfully, there is no sense in paying for something which is never read. Encourage your staff to read them. Look to see if there is a cheaper online subscription. If it remains unused, cancel the subscription.

151. Stop sending stamped addressed envelopes

Postage is remarkably cheap in the UK. Visit almost any other country, try to send a letter, and you will immediately see what good value Royal Mail is. However, this has led many charities to include stamped addressed envelopes automatically whenever they want a response from someone.

In some cases, such as a donation request, this is a good idea because it encourages response, but in most cases it is an unnecessary expense – the recipient will think nothing of putting a stamp on it themselves. It costs them a few pennies, while over a year the total cost of all these stamped addressed envelopes easily can run into hundreds of pounds.

... over a year the total cost of stamped addressed envelopes can run into hundreds of pounds.

152. Get cheaper postage

Postage costs can add up, so look into a service such as ViaPost. This service allows anyone to send physical post directly from a computer to any UK address. By removing the cost of printing, stationery and delivery, and charging just 27p + VAT per letter, it promises savings of around 25 per cent on traditional mail. You can download the free software at: www.viapost.com.

153. Use scrap paper for notepads

Stop spending money on notepads. Instead, collect scrap paper, and once a month, cut it up, staple it together and make your own pads.

154. Reduce paper use

According to the government environmental agency Envirowise, the average office worker in the UK gets through an astonishing 50 sheets of A4 paper every day. Furthermore, paper usage is rising by around 20 per cent every year. If you are wasteful with paper, you easily could be getting through 100 sheets per day per employee. Envirowise believes that it is possible to cut this to just 15 a day by following these steps:

- issue documents electronically rather than in paper form
- encourage employees to think about whether they need to print a document.

Set your printer to print on both sides of the paper...

Set your printer to print on both sides of the paper by default.

155. Buy cheaper paper

As well as reducing the amount of paper that you consume, you can cut your expenditure on paper by reducing what you pay for each sheet. There are two simple steps to achieving this: first, buy thinner paper of 80gsm; second, buy recycled paper.

Some people might complain that thinner, recycled paper is of lower quality than they are used to, but this should only matter if you have important documents that need to last for a long time. Perhaps consider buying some higher quality paper for those occasions, but for everyday use, 80gsm recycled paper should be more than acceptable.

...for everyday use, 80gsm recycled paper should be more than acceptable.

156. Have a disaster recovery plan

What would you do if your premises were destroyed by fire, flood or some other catastrophe? What if you suddenly and tragically lost one of your key personnel, or if terrorist action affected your operations?

Think it sounds like the plot of a far-fetched film? Well, these things do happen – and they could happen to you. You need to have a disaster recovery plan in place to make sure that you can get your organisation up and running again with minimal disruption and cost. The contents of this plan will vary from organisation to organisation, but it should cover key personnel, facilities and external communication. Who will be in charge? Where will they operate from, and how will they communicate with the outside world?

Write a simple plan and make sure that all the relevant people know what it is. If the worst does happen, it could save your organisation vast sums of money. It could even enable your charity to survive.

Write a simple plan and make sure all the relevant people know what it is.

157. Stop giving away free plastic bags

We all know the damage that plastic bags do. If you are not yet aware of this, here are a few facts that should make you think:

- in the UK, we use 167 bags per person each year
- on average, each single-use plastic bag is discarded within 20 minutes
- a plastic bag will take between 15 and 1,000 years to break down in the environment
- more than 100,000 birds and marine animals die each year as a result of plastic
- the petrol used to make a single-use plastic bag is enough to drive a car 115 miles.

All this matters, of course, and this is why more and more shoppers decline the offer of free plastic bags in shops. However, if you run a shop, you will be acutely aware of how much they cost you to give away to shoppers. Why not follow the example of the National Trust, which in 2008 started to charge 5p per plastic bag? Within six months it had cut the number of bags that it handed out by 95 per cent.

Why not start charging 5p per plastic bag?

Chapter 11

Utilities

158. Know much gas and electricity you use

Bills for gas and electricity can be very difficult to understand. However, with energy becoming so expensive, it is vital that you get an accurate picture of where you stand. Without that knowledge you cannot hope to reduce your spending in this area. So, take some time to understand your bill. If necessary, call your supplier and ask for a detailed breakdown of usage.

... take some time to understand your bill.

Many suppliers now offer energy-usage monitors. You attach these to your meters, and they send data on energy usage to your computer, so you can see exactly what you are using and when. At the time of writing, the power and gas company E.ON was carrying out a trial with the regulator Ofgem to monitor how customers change their usage with one of these monitors installed. Early results indicated that, on average, customers were able to reduce their consumption by more than 5 per cent.

159. Get the best price for your energy

Whichever supplier you use for your gas or electricity, it will look the same, and will do the same job – but its cost may vary significantly. If you have not switched from your automatic regional supplier you almost certainly are paying too much for your energy – perhaps by as much as 25 per cent. So, shop around. Visit an online comparison site. These offer consumer prices but will give you an

Visit an online comparison site.

indication of which providers to contact for a commercial price.

160. Watch the international oil markets

Andrew Lees of cost-reduction consultancy Expense Reduction Analysts has worked with charities such as the British Lung Foundation and the Royal British Legion, helping them to cut costs. He offers this advice on how to get cheap energy:

> *Keep a close eye on the international oil markets. There's been enormous fluctuation in them in recent years, and if you could get a fixed-price energy deal when they're at a low, you'll end up paying a great deal less than if you go to the market when prices are high.*

...get a fixed-price energy deal when they're at a low...

161. Switch off computers at night

As well as reducing the amount that you spend per unit of energy, you can reduce your actual energy consumption. If computers are left on standby, they still use 50 per cent of the electricity that they use when they are on. Not only is this damaging to the environment, it is also costing you money. So, encourage your staff to switch off their computers when they leave the office.

You might find that it is enough to inform your staff about the waste, and explain to them what it could mean to the charity and to them individually if everyone switched off their PCs before they leave. However, most organisations find that this is not enough to actually change behaviour.

So, why not make one person in every office responsible for turning them off at the end of every day, or run spot checks and highlight offenders? Or be positive about it – run spot checks and award prizes to those who consistently turn them off over three months.

...encourage your staff to switch off their computers when they leave the office.

There are many ways to encourage this environmentally-friendly and cost-conscious behaviour. Getting it right will not save you millions of pounds, but it will shave a few pounds off your annual electricity bill.

162. Use energy-efficient lightbulbs

The traditional lightbulb has not altered for more than a century, and it wastes 95 per cent of electricity as heat. To avoid this waste, you need to switch to energy-efficient lightbulbs, also known as compact fluorescent lights.

According to the Energy Saving Trust, compact fluorescent lightbulbs last up to 10 times longer than traditional bulbs. Just one energy-saving bulb could save up to £7 a year and, depending on the length of time that lights are in use everyday, could save around £60 before it needs to be replaced.

...just one energy-saving bulb could save up to £7 a year.

Look around the room you are in now. How many traditional bulbs are in this room? How many rooms are in your building? How many buildings does your charity operate? So, roughly how many bulbs do you have? If you save £7 a year on each one, that could be a fairly impressive saving.

Energy-efficient bulbs have come on a long way in the last few years, and you can buy them now in many retailers for under £1. The economic case is unarguable, as is the environmental one. So, what is stopping you?

163. Place foil sheeting behind your radiators

Adding a sheet of foil to the back of your radiator will reflect heat back into the room and prevent it from escaping through the walls. Be prepared for a few strange looks when you arrive with a roll of foil paper and a ball of Blu Tack, but the embarrassment will be worth it when you can reduce the thermostat by one degree, still keeping the building warm, and saving yet more money on your heating bills.

164. Fit draught excluders yourself

Fitting draught excluders to your doors and windows is one of the most effective ways of reducing your heating bills. You may have been meaning to get around to getting them fitted but put it off because you weren't sure just how much you would save on your bills, and because you were worried about the cost.

The amount that fitting draught excluders will save on your heating bill depends on how draughty your building is, how efficient your heating system is, and how cold the weather is. You cannot be sure how much it will save, but you can be sure that it will save you something.

You would be right about the cost of paying someone to fit them, though. So why not fit them yourself? The simplest draught excluders are just self-adhesive foam-plastic strips. Go to your local hardware shop, buy a length of strip, cut it to the length required, peel off the backing tape, and press it into place. What could be easier? Or, if you are genuinely DIY-averse, is there someone else in your organisation who could do this?

The simplest draught excluders are just self-adhesive foam-plastic strips.

However, remember that, as with all DIY work, there are risks involved. For example, it would be possible, if unlikely, for someone to fall through a window that is large enough. So, before you do any of this, conduct a risk assessment (see www.hse.gov.uk for a straightforward method).

165. Cut down on water waste

Gas and electricity are not the only utilities you can save money on – you can get cheaper water, and use less of it.

A 5mm stream of water wastes 528,000 litres of water each year...

By following these steps, you could see you office water bills shrink by 30 per cent.

- Make sure that employees turn off taps fully – a 5mm stream of water wastes 528,000 litres of water each year, costing up to £705.
- Fit a water displacement bag – most water companies will supply these for free, or you can simply place a 1 litre plastic bottle filled with water into the toilet cistern to reduce the amount of water used with every flush.
- Check pipes for leaks – these not only add to your water bill, they also damage your building.

166. Buy tax-efficient water-saving devices

In the March 2001 Budget, the Government announced support for business investment in environmentally friendly technologies under the Green Technology Challenge. This allows for the introduction of a 100 per cent first-year Enhanced Capital Allowance scheme on technologies to save, and improve the quality of, water.

The Water Technology Product List, which is updated each month, details the eligible products and, in some cases, the amounts which can be claimed when the product is incorporated in a larger piece of equipment. (See: www.eca-water.gov.uk.)

Chapter 12

Equipment

167. Know what you own

It is remarkable how few organisations actually know what they own. Individual managers buy kit, and there is no central record kept of it. Departments are merged or relocated, and expensive pieces of equipment end up lost in a storeroom somewhere. It is a common situation – and it's very likely that there is under-used equipment hiding somewhere in your operation too.

If you want to cut equipment costs, the first step is to pull together a central register of what you own. This will give you a clear picture of how you can save money in at least two ways: what you can sell to raise cash, and what you need to buy to make your operation run more efficiently.

...pull together a central register of what you own.

168. Sell off unnecessary equipment

How much equipment do you have that you no longer need? Old computers taking up space in a cupboard, office furniture that you replaced a year ago but have not quite got round to moving out of the storeroom, or just piles of out-of-date marketing materials.

If this sounds familiar, then you need to take action. Round up everything which your charity is holding on to that it no longer needs. Sort it into two piles: one of items that you could sell, and the other of rubbish. Just by disposing of the second pile, you will be saving yourself money by freeing up space that you will be able to use productively.

...make valuable revenue for your charity by selling your unnecessary equipment.

Then, you can make valuable revenue for your charity by selling your unnecessary equipment. Try selling it back to the original supplier, or call local organisations that you think might be interested. Failing that, you can always put it in the local paper or auction it on eBay (www.ebay.co.uk).

169. Replace old equipment that is expensive to run

Every workplace has one. The old piece of kit which has been around for longer than anyone cares to remember. In some workplaces it is a printer that takes an age to chug out blotchy, crumpled documents. In others it is an alarm that goes off by mistake once a month, meaning that you have to keep calling out the keyholding company.

If you have one of these items, you may have agreed with the general consensus that it would be nice to replace it but you just don't have the money right now. Anyway, it is not that bad – you just need to know where to hit it and how hard to get it working.

...you might find that you would be better off buying new equipment.

However, think for a minute about how expensive that old piece of equipment is to run. How much less ink and paper would a new printer use? How much are you spending on call-out fees? Add it all up, and you might find that you would be better off buying new equipment. Remember that the option with the lowest initial outlay is not always the cheapest in the long run.

170. Ask people to donate equipment

Before you rush out to your local IKEA, chequebook in hand, consider a few alternatives. You would be surprised at what people have that they are willing to give away. Before you spend any money on new equipment, ask people you know if they can donate it to you. Try other charities, local businesses, your local authority, friends and family. Get into the habit of mentioning it whenever you meet someone new.

171. Buy damaged office furniture

The physical working environment in your organisation can have a huge effect on the productivity of your staff. Inspiring spaces that are full of natural light are the best places for developing ideas. Getting furniture that looks good and feels comfortable can make all the difference. However, it also can be extremely expensive.

There is a way of getting smart, functional furniture from top suppliers without paying an exorbitant amount for it. Visit them and ask for damaged items. Often, you will be able to get a desk with a scratch down one side, a filing cabinet with a small dent in it, or a bookcase with a mark on the back for a fraction of the price that you would pay for the same item without those minor flaws.

...ask top suppliers for damaged items.

Then, when you get it back to the office, simply arrange the furniture to cover up any noticeable damage. It will look as good as new – and you will have an office that looks a million dollars, having only spent a few hundred pounds!

172. Hire equipment rather than buying

It is shockingly common for organisations to buy expensive equipment that they only use a few times a year, and which for the rest of the time sits idle. Many items need replacing in five years' time anyway. This means that something that cost thousands of pounds may be used only 10 or 20 times, when it would have cost a fraction of that figure to hire it at the times when it was needed. So, consider hiring rather than buying for all future equipment purchases.

...consider hiring rather than buying for all future equipment purchases.

You can save money right now by auditing your existing major equipment. Look at each item in turn. Work out how many times you will use it before you need to replace it, research how much it would cost to hire it that many times, and find out how much you could sell it for – if you can get more for selling it than it would cost you to hire a replacement, then do so.

173. Reduce noise levels

Not only would most responsible employers want to look after their staff, increasingly they are recognising that it is cost-efficient to do so. A safe working environment leads to fewer days off work through injury, illness and stress, and it improves productivity when those employees are in the office. For example, most organisations now ensure that employees have a comfortable chair, that their posture is good and that they have adequate light. Yet they often overlook one area of employee health: their hearing.

. . . excess noise can contribute to increased stress levels and lower productivity.

Few organisations realise that excess noise, caused by a combination of voices, printers, fax machines and mobile phones all at once, can contribute to increased stress levels and lower productivity. In an attempt to address this, the European Union brought in the Noise at Work regulation in 2006. This stipulates that employers must implement safety measures to keep daily average sound exposure below 85 decibels for their employees.

Most organisations find this law confusing, difficult to implement and impossible to measure. As a result, they often ignore it. However, this can lead to unnecessary costs, such as increased absence, reduced productivity and higher staff turnover. The telephony provider GN Netcom has come up with the following seven tips for avoiding these costs.

1. **Design your office layout carefully.** Sitting in front of a photocopier or fax machine that is constantly beeping to inform you that it is out of paper would irritate even the calmest individual. So, think about

your office layout. Consider placing all office appliances at the back of the office, or in another room, so that no one can hear them.

2. **Choose an appropriate headset.** If you work in a busy and noisy environment, being on the phone can be quite difficult. A duo headset reduces background noise and ensures a crystal-clear conversation, by directing sound into both ears of the phone user. This means that employees are focused fully on calls, and the general noise level in your office is lower.

3. **Reduce time on the phone.** Consider how many hours your employees spend on the phone. Noise coming across the phone system is a main source of noise exposure, and in the long run can be physically and psychologically harmful.

4. **Go wireless.** Provide wireless headsets. These enable staff to take conference calls or other lengthy conversations away from their desk, thereby improving the work environment for others as well as themselves.

5. **The softer the better.** Replace wood flooring with carpet, and introduce some plants to help absorb ambient noise.

6. **Separation is good.** Establish a separate room for all meetings, and ask staff to take all group conversations to a separate area.

7. **Shhh!** Tell all employees to switch their phones off if they are away from their desk for some time.

174. Look out for businesses going bust

Companies that are going out of business usually have to sell their assets to pay the people to whom they owe money. This gives you the opportunity to buy their equipment at knock-down prices. Keep an eye on the local media, look for advertisements announcing these sales, and try to be in the right place at the right time. Finally, be prepared to transport the equipment yourself.

...be in the right place at the right time.

Chapter 13

Fleet

175. Manage your fleet

Not every voluntary organisation operates a fleet, but if you do have one, it is likely to be a significant expense and one which has grown rapidly in recent years. Whether it is a minibus, a handful of company cars or a nationwide fleet of vans, your fleet is an essential part of your operation, and you need to find some ways of controlling spiralling costs.

...many organisations could save 10 per cent on every company car by managing their fleets more effectively.

Global finance provider GE Capital has estimated that many organisations could save 10 per cent on every single company car just by managing their fleets more effectively. Its *Car Policy Survey 2008* examined 170,000 vehicles being run by 700 businesses across Europe, and found that opportunities to cut costs existed in a wide range of areas. For example, the organisations could save an annual average of £170 per car through better fuel management, and an annual average of £220 per car by capping CO_2 emissions to reduce insurance, Vehicle Excise Duty and fuel costs.

176. Invest in fleet management software

...consider investing in software that will do much of the time-consuming work for you...

Running a vehicle fleet is time-consuming, but if it has the potential to make significant savings, then it needs to be done. But do consider investing in software that will do much of the time-consuming work for you and help you make even greater savings.

You can buy software that will track vehicles while they are on the road and ensure that they are all used to maximum efficiency. In addition, you can track mileage, petrol consumption and many other factors – by vehicle, and by driver. The software will remind you when vehicles are due for services, when tax needs to be paid, and so on. This should ensure that repairs are done before problems arise.

(For examples, look at: www.jaama.co.uk, www.bluecs. co.uk and www.tracesystems.co.uk.)

177. Sell underused vehicles

Look at what each vehicle in your fleet is used for, and how much time it spends idling in a garage. You might find that you can sell one or more of your vehicles without any adverse effect on the organisation. Plan to review your vehicle requirements on a regular basis.

178. Buy smaller, cheaper vehicles

Next time you need to invest in a new vehicle for your fleet, instead of replacing like for like, or buying a new vehicle of the same size, make and model as your existing one, look into buying a slightly cheaper model. Vehicles are expensive, so if you can trim just 5 per cent from the purchase price, you are saving a lot of money. Unless you go for something that is dramatically cheaper, the drivers in your organisation are unlikely to notice the difference. Choose carefully, and they even may prefer the new vehicle.

... if you can trim just 5 per cent from the purchase price, you are saving a lot of money.

However, remember to consider the total cost of the vehicle. Don't look just at the headline price. Consider the costs of insurance, tax, maintenance, fuel and, of course, the rate of depreciation.

Buy fuel-efficient cars, and you could cut your fuel bill by up to 25 per cent.

179. Shift to fuel-efficient cars

Buy fuel-efficient cars, and you could cut your organisation's annual fuel bill by up to 25 per cent. Consider whether you could use smaller cars, whether diesel would be a better option than petrol, and even whether a hybrid car would meet your needs. Most new cars carry a colour-coded fuel-efficiency badge, with Band A cars emitting the least CO_2, and Band G cars the most.

For more information on buying a fuel-efficient car, and to see how your current vehicles stack up, go to this government information website: http://campaigns.direct. gov.uk/actonco2/home/on-the-move/buying-your-car.html.

180. Join a car club

In recent years a number of car clubs have sprung up, offering consumers an affordable and convenient alternative to car ownership. At the time of writing, companies such as Streetcar, City Car Club and WhizzGo charged an annual membership fee of around £30 per driver, and around £5 an hour (including petrol) or £25 per day. You simply turn up to where the car is parked, enter your code and go. If one of their sites is near your offices, this could be a much cheaper option than taking taxis or company cars.

... car clubs could be a much cheaper option than taxis or company cars.

181. Encourage fuel-efficient driving

If you maintain a fleet of vehicles or have staff who travel a lot, you will know what an expense fuel can be. However, you might not be aware of just how much you can cut that expense by encouraging more fuel-efficient driving. By driving more smoothly you can cut your spending on fuel by a remarkable 60 per cent. What is more, you can achieve this without increasing your journey times, by simply following these tips.

- **Don't accelerate too dramatically.** Over-revving uses more fuel, so if you accelerate more gradually, keeping under 3,000 revs, you will save money.
- **Drive in the correct gear.** Always drive in the highest gear possible without labouring the engine.
- **Easy on the brakes.** Let your car slow down naturally and smoothly.
- **Use air conditioning sparingly.** It significantly increases fuel consumption.
- **Drive away immediately when starting from cold.** Idling to heat the engine wastes fuel and causes rapid engine wear.
- **Remove roof racks when not in use.** They increase drag significantly.
- **Avoid short journeys.** A cold engine uses almost twice as much fuel as a warm one.
- **Drive more slowly.** Driving at 85mph rather than 70mph uses 25 per cent more fuel.
- **If you are stuck in a traffic jam, switch off.** Cutting the engine will save fuel and stop emissions.
- **Keep tyres properly inflated.** You can improve your fuel efficiency by 3 per cent just by having your car's tyres properly inflated, so make sure that the tyres are regularly tested.

Air conditioning significantly increases fuel consumption.

By encouraging your drivers to follow these tips, you could slash your fuel costs very quickly. As oil prices fluctuate and fuel tax increases, this is a cost-saving area that will become more and more important to the cost-conscious organisation.

182. Buy the cheapest petrol in your area

At the free website www.petrolprices.com you can input your postcode and state how far you are willing to travel to fill your tank, and the site will tell you where to find the cheapest fuel in that area. It is not unusual to find variations of 5 per cent from one forecourt to the next. How much would that save you every year?

183. Monitor drivers through fuel cards

If you want to be sure that your organisation's drivers are filling up at the cheapest forecourts, and are taking on board your advice about fuel efficiency, consider giving them fuel cards. These show you to see exactly where they have been filling up, and will enable you to monitor their usage compared to their mileage. This should highlight serious offenders so that you can address the issue with them. It also removes the need for a time-consuming and administration-heavy process for refunding petrol purchases.

...fuel cards enable you to monitor usage compared to mileage.

184. Do basic vehicle maintenance yourself

Most of us tend to be wary of having anything to do with our cars beyond switching them on, pointing them in the right direction and pushing the pedals at the right time. Once a year, we take them in for an MOT and a service and let the experts take care of the maintenance.

For the most part, this is a very sensible policy. Modern cars are so complicated and so dependent on electronics that often, maintenance is best left to a specialist. However, there are a few things that you can do yourself, not in order to reduce your expenditure on professional maintenance – that is still essential – but to minimise the number of breakdowns that your fleet suffers.

...there are a few things that you can do yourself to minimise breakdowns...

You may have someone in your organisation who knows their way around vehicles and so will be ideally suited to this work. You even might want to consider including it in their job description. Remember, however, that anything that is in any way dangerous should be done by a fully trained and qualified professional (see tip 321).

185. Check oil frequently

Check the oil in your vehicles regularly. By the time the warning light on the dashboard has come on it is often too late, and damage may have been done to the engine already. You might even need to shell out for a new engine. So, simply get hold of the dipstick, pop it in the oil, and check that it is topped up sufficiently. Always ensure that the engine is off before doing this.

...get hold of the dipstick, pop it in the oil, and check that it is topped up...

186. Monitor coolant levels

The coolant in the engine does what you might expect – it cools the engine. If it runs out, your engine will overheat and you could have to pay for a new one. Avoid this hefty bill by keeping an eye on coolant levels.

Much of the liquid is inside the radiator. Never open this when the engine is hot, as the pressure in the system can send hot coolant splashing out on to you. In most cars, the coolant is visible as an orange liquid in a transparent bottle with level markings. Keep the coolant between these markings, and only open it to top it up when the engine is cold.

187. Know when to change your timing belt

This piece of car maintenance does not even involve opening a bonnet. In fact, you can do it from the comfort of your desk. It is to know when to change your timing belt. Too many people only know that their timing belt needs changing when their engine goes dead one day.

Too many people only know that their timing belt needs changing when their engine goes dead...

They then have to pay for their car to be towed to the mechanics, and any costs for alternative travel, as well as the cost of the replacement belt.

Belts need to be changed every 50,000–70,000 miles, depending on the make of car. While you don't want to pay for a new belt that has 20,000 miles left in it, equally you don't want to be lumbered with emergency costs on top of paying for a new timing belt.

How do you know when your belt needs changing? Simply contact the manufacturer of your car, or visit a website such as www.familycar.com, which allows you to download a document listing most makes and models of car, together with the mileage at which the belt needs to be replaced.

188. Check that your cooling fan is working

These days it is rarely worthwhile to repair an engine...

A broken cooling fan is a common cause of engine overheating. These days it is rarely worthwhile to repair an engine, so engine damage can lead to a large bill for a new one.

The cooling fan only comes on when you are driving below 20 miles per hour. Above that level, enough air passes through the engine to keep it cool. However, if you rarely get stuck in traffic below this speed, the only way you will find out whether the fan is broken is when you are suddenly stuck in traffic, the fan does not come on, and the engine overheats.

So, start your car, and leave it running until it reaches operating temperature. At some point you should hear the cooling fan start. If it does start, then it is broken and you need to get it replaced.

189. Simplify your fuel claims process

If your staff use their own vehicles for business travel, they will want to claim back the cost of doing so. Many organisations devise remarkably complex systems for doing this. The time that it takes managers and staff to work through these processes can become a drain on the organisation's resources. It is far better to use a simple system, even if it does result in paying a little more to staff.

190. Insist on receipts for mileage claims

According to specialist expenses provider GlobalExpense, around 40 per cent of mileage claims are not accompanied by a receipt. As a consequence, you could be missing out on thousands of pounds of recoverable VAT.

In one year, the average expense-claiming employee will have claimed £49.32 for business mileage, as well as spending £185 on flights and making about 2.4 train journeys at an average cost of £42.06.

Your policy should be simple: no receipt, no claim.

...you could be missing out on thousands of pounds of recoverable VAT.

103

Chapter 14

Information technology

191. Streamline your IT systems

As organisations grow, they tend to build up a haphazard collection of IT systems. New servers are tacked on to older ones, unused desktops start functioning as servers, and mysterious cabling runs through boxes which have an indeterminate function but which no one is sufficiently confident to cut out of the system.

These IT systems resemble old houses which have been built by generation after generation of owner with no masterplan. These houses tend to be inefficient and wasteful of resources, and the chances are that your IT system is no different.

Task your IT expert with designing a new system with as little hardware as possible.

Task your IT expert with designing a new system that does exactly what you require, with minimal resources and as little hardware as possible. You are likely to end up with a system that uses fewer resources, requires less maintenance, and delivers a better service to its users.

192. Share IT costs

Charityshare (www.charityshare.org.uk) is a consortium IT venture jointly owned by the NSPCC, the Children's Society and the Alzheimer's Society. It provides, manages and supports the charities' IT infrastructure and associated IT services, and has led to a reduction of 25 per cent in the unit costs of the IT equipment and services used by the 4,000 employees of those three charities.

Annual savings to the participating charities are now running at more than £1 million a year. Charityshare demonstrates that innovative and successful collaborative working between charities to the benefit of those that the charities serve is practical, effective and economical.

So, why not set up your own scheme? Find charities that have similar IT requirements to yours, ask Charityshare for advice on how it operates, and see if you too can drive down your IT costs.

...innovative and successful collaborative working between charities is practical, effective and economical.

193. Use the Charity Technology Exchange

Would you like to save between 92 per cent and 96 per cent on the cost of around 170 technology products from the likes of Microsoft, Cisco and Symantec? For example, would a copy of Office Accounting Pro, adapted by Microsoft so that it covers all the requisite charity accounting stipulations, at that sort of discount be of interest? If not, then this probably isn't the book for you!

...save between 92 per cent and 96 per cent on the cost of around 170 technology products...

The Charity Technology Trust, in partnership with the not-for-profit technology capacity-building organisation TechSoup, has banded together with technology providers to offer these products to charities at no cost other than a small administrative fee for running the scheme.

There really is no catch. The fact is that most charities do not know about the scheme, and are spending thousands of pounds every year on technology products that they can get free of charge.

Congratulations – you now know about it. Go to www.ctxchange.org to register and start receiving your products.

194. Find a free solution to spam

The St Martin's Centre for Health and Healing, a charity based in Birmingham's famous Bull Ring, faced significant problems with spam email. IT manager Tom Thompson explains:

> We were getting hundreds and hundreds of spam emails a week. It was a huge nuisance to filter, and some of it was very distressing in content for our staff and volunteers. We looked at some commercial solutions, but the figures involved were out of the question.

This is a common financial reality for an organisation of this size. Thompson freely admits that the centre struggles. Even where counselling is provided at a cost to the charity of around £30 per session, users are invited to pay only what they can afford, on an anonymous basis. However, with Mailshell's Anti-Spam Desktop now available by donation on the Charity Technology Exchange (CTX) programme, the charity's spam issues have all but disappeared overnight.

Thompson is keen to stress the value of CTX and its donor partners to charities such as St Martin's, and is very appreciative of their help: 'Without CTX we could never have afforded this sort of solution,' he says.

195. Ask your IT consultants for free products

... external advisers can be a goldmine of free or cheap alternatives to costly items...

Your external advisers can be a goldmine of free or cheap alternatives to costly items, but very often it just will not occur to them to tell you about what they know. So ask them. Childhood First did to spectacular effect.

Childhood First's finance and administration director Mark O'Kelly, says:

> It was our IT consultants who told me about the Charity Technology Exchange – a scheme that offers software to

charities at minimal cost. This led to us acquiring a Microsoft donation of server and Office software that will go towards the goal of improving facilities and communication throughout the organisation.

196. Get free software

You would be amazed how many free alternatives there are to the expensive software you can buy. For examples, see: www.download.com, www.brothersoft.com and www.free serifsoftware.com.

If you don't find what you are looking for there, before you spend hundreds of pounds on new software, try the publisher's website – they usually have free trial versions which can last for up to three months.

197. Don't pay for anti-virus software

Online viruses can be expensive. Some can cripple your IT systems, reducing your organisation's activity for days and days. Others can wipe your hard drives, meaning that you lose vital data. Without doubt, they are best avoided. That is why many charities spend as much as they possibly can on antivirus software. However, each licence can cost £50, so if you have 12 employees you can spend £600 without noticing it.

Eliminate this expenditure in one fell swoop by downloading free software, which you can find with a simple online search. This software performs all the same functions as the leading anti-virus software, and all your staff can download it to their computers in a matter of minutes. Best of all, it costs absolutely nothing.

. . . download free software, which you can find with a simple online search.

198. Automate personnel and payroll records

... an online personnel and payroll system means that line managers can do it themselves.

During 2009, the children's charity Action for Children (formerly NCH) introduced an online personnel and payroll system for its 6,500 employees. Previously, the charity had two separate systems for personnel and payroll records, so the HR department had to input information twice. The new system means that line managers can do it themselves. It also means that the information only needs to be inputted once. This will reduce errors and reduce the organisation's need for an expensive HR resource.

These software solutions can cost thousands of pounds, but Action for Children expects that it will lead to significant cost reductions. You too could save money in this way – why not look into it today?

199. Keep off-site back-ups

The Aid and Assist Project is a small charity which helps disadvantaged families in East Anglia. In February 2009, it was told to repay £185,000 to the European Social Fund after a flood left it unable to provide documentation on how it had spent the funding that it received.

A flood at the charity's workshop in 2006 destroyed invoices showing how the money was spent, so it was unable to prove to auditors where the funding had gone. On 14 January, the organisation received a letter from the Government Office for the East of England asking it to repay the whole amount within one month. Project manager Ann Stockdale-Bond said that the organisation was unable to pay back the funds, and would be forced to close if the European Social Fund insisted on the return of the money.

What would you do if this happened to you? What would you do if you lost all your payroll details, your donor contact database, or your financial records?

To ensure that you are safe even in the worst-case scenario, make sure you keep an offsite back-up of this vital data. There are now many companies offering online back-ups. These cost no more than a few pounds per month, are easy to set up and, once they are set up, run automatically. Begin by identifying your business-critical data, then set up an online back-up. Do it now. It could save you thousands of pounds in the future. It could even keep your charity operating.

. . . make sure you keep an offsite back-up of vital data.

200. Use cloud computing

Cloud computing is really a very simple concept, and it could be saving your organisation a lot of money right now. Cloud computing is a system in which software and services are delivered over the Web and through a browser. Users of cloud computing do not need to have their own servers or software, they can access their documents and programmes whenever they want, from anywhere in the world where they can get online.

This allows organisations such as yours to run pretty much all their needs on the Internet, paying just a small monthly fee, rather than paying large upfront costs for hardware and software. Take a look into what it can do for you.

201. Use free wireless Internet locations

A cheap way to get online when out of the office is to use free wireless Internet locations. Most laptops now have wireless capability built into them. All you need to do is switch it on, and then if you are within range of a free signal you can connect with just a couple of clicks.

For example, McDonalds now offers free wireless within its restaurants. A small coffee in McDonalds costs around £1, so if your staff are only connecting a handful of times a month it makes sense for them to do this rather than pay for a mobile Internet contract.

(To find free wireless hotspots, see: www.myhotspots. co.uk.)

Chapter 15

Telecommunications

202. Get phone and broadband from the same provider

In recent years the cost of phone and broadband packages has tumbled. If you are still on a contract from before 2008, you are wasting money. In fact, by finding the cheapest provider and taking both phone and broadband from the same provider, you should be able to halve the amount you spend on what is now a fairly inexpensive utility.

If you are still on a contract from before 2008, you are wasting money.

203. Switch to an Internet-based phone service

If you have not switched your phone system to Voice over Internet Protocol (VoIP) already then you almost certainly can save money by doing so. With VoIP you transmit your voice calls over your broadband line rather than through a traditional telephone exchange. Because the broadband line is already there, it costs the service provider very little to enable voice transmission, and so it is cheaper.

The VoIP market is growing rapidly, so often providers will offer discounts to organisations setting up an account. At the very least you should get free features such as three-way conferencing, call waiting and caller identification.

...transmit your voice calls over broadband rather than a traditional telephone exchange.

204. Switch mobile phone provider

Like most new technologies, the cost of mobile phone calls has fallen over time, so make sure that you are on the best contract available. Shop around and get quotes from alternative providers.

Don't forget to ask your existing provider to give you a price...

Don't forget to ask your existing provider to give you a price too. There are so few new customers available to these companies that they are desperate to keep the customers that they do have. They should be willing to give you an excellent deal.

205. Don't use your mobile phone to connect to the Internet

Once upon a time, if you were out and about at a meeting, you were cut off from the office. Then the mobile came along, and we found that we could catch up on missed calls or important events wherever we were. However, once we could use them to access the Internet, we discovered that they charged an inordinate amount.

The dongle is a great step forward for anyone who is often on the move.

The best solution to this comes in the shape of the dongle – a piece of kit that you plug into your laptop, usually through the USB port, which allows you to use a mobile phone network to connect to the Internet. These have proved a great step forward for anyone who is often on the move. To access your emails or look something up on the Internet, all you need to do is open your laptop, connect through your dongle, and you're away.

As well as being very easy, contracts for this form of mobile Internet cost a fraction of what it costs to get online through a mobile phone. Most people do not need to spend more than £10 a month on it. So if you have a few members of staff who are often out and about, and are racking up major bills on their mobile phones, contact your mobile phone providers and get onto one of these tariffs.

206. Get cheap, recycled mobile phones

Every month, millions of mobile phone handsets which are still in perfectly good working condition are discarded and sent to Britain's growing landfill sites as mobile phone fashions come and go. However, for shoppers who are more eco-conscious than fashion-conscious, there is now an alternative to filling the UK's landfill sites that is also a great way for charities to save money.

The company www.purplegossip.com offers a wide range of recycled phones and accessories. Phones are available for up to 60 per cent off the original price, with phones from as little as £10 and accessories from as little as 99p, plus free delivery on orders over £100. All product packaging and box inserts are made from recycled materials. Delivery is within three working days.

Because there are no contracts involved, this is a particularly good option if a member of staff loses their mobile phone. By choosing a recycled replacement not only will you be prolonging the life cycle of the handset and actively helping to reduce the amount of hazardous waste in Britain's landfills, but you will be trimming your bills too.

By choosing a recycled replacement you will be trimming your bills.

207. Say no to 0870

Companies set up 0870 numbers not because they are easier for you to remember, but because the company makes money every time you call them – and you foot the bill. The amount that you pay varies, but while many phone packages have an all-inclusive package for local numbers that begin with 01, you could be paying 5p per minute for an 0870 number.

Encourage your staff to stop before dialling 0870 and to visit the website www.saynoto0870.com. This has a very simple search function. You type in the 0870 number that you want to avoid, and the site gives you the local 01 version. The site is run by volunteers, and the data is provided by users, so it may not be able to give you an alternative, but in the long run it will make a difference to your phone bills.

... type in the 0870 number you want to avoid, and the site gives you the local 01 version.

On the other hand, if you have commercial organisations calling you, or you provide a phone service for people who can afford it, you might want to consider setting up your own 0870 number. You will not make huge sums of money from it, but it can add a handy few pounds to your coffers every month.

208. Cut the cost of calling abroad

You have shopped around to get the best phone deal for your organisation, and are glad to see that your monthly bills have fallen, but when you look through them, you still see high cost calls. On closer inspection, you discover that these are to overseas numbers.

This might not be a problem for your organisation. You might operate solely within the UK, in which case you will not have any problems in this area. However, if your staff do need to make overseas calls, you will be glad to learn that there is a simple and entire legal way of slashing the cost of international calls.

... if your staff need to make overseas calls, sign up to an override service.

Simply sign up to an override service. These require you to dial a number before the number you want to call, and then to listen to a short message before being connected: they can decimate the rates that you pay for international calls. For example, costs to countries such as the United States can be reduced to as little as 0.5p.

209. Simplify your billing

Managing telecommunications for an organisation with projects spread around the country can be can be a difficult business. For Hafal, a mental health charity with 63 projects across Wales, telecoms billing was becoming a major administrative challenge.

Hafal works with individuals recovering from severe mental illness, and its 112 staff and 150 volunteers provide support to more than 640 people a day across Wales. As the organisation has grown, it has added new telecommunications suppliers as and when required. Within a few years, the situation had become complicated.

Head of finance Barbara Richards says:

Our supplier was sending some bills to individual sites and other bills direct to head office. They were coming in at different times during the quarter, and the lack of uniformity was proving a real headache. We also weren't being given a great of support or advice in terms of tidying up our telecoms and billing.

Richards decided to consolidate all the charity's telecommunications into one supplier, and chose Class Telecommunications. She reports that this decision has helped her to save money:

The billing is now much more efficient, and staff from Class have visited us every month to review the bills and advise us on where we can make further efficiency savings. We have saved a lot of money with them.

Of course, Class Telecommunications is not the only company that offers these services. A simple online search will reveal many others. Take a look now and see if you can save as much money as Hafal did.

... consolidate all your telecommunications into one supplier ...

210. Get your phone bills professionally checked

... up to 80 per cent of all telecommunications bills contain errors...

Often, telecommunications costs can be one of the top three administration costs of any charity. According to telecommunications expense management specialist Veropath, up to 80 per cent of all telecoms bills contain errors, and most organisations are not on the best tariff or plan from their providers.

You can save money by employing a telecommunications expense management firm to check your bills, compare different tariffs, and select the optimum set of providers for your organisation. These organisations check each bill against the agreement from the supplier before approving it for payment. They also check that costs match activities.

For example, how much do you spend on fundraising calls, and which individuals and teams are the most effective? How much does it cost to run your free helpline? Veropath estimates that organisations can save between 30 and 50 per cent on their annual telecommunications costs by getting their phone bills checked in this way.

Chapter 16

Printing

211. Encourage staff to cut down on print

Most of us print far more than we need to. You can encourage staff to make inroads into your print and ink costs by asking them to:

- stop and think before printing something. Does it need to be printed? Do you need to print the entire document?
- proofread documents carefully so that you don't have to reprint if you spot a typo
- use the onscreen print preview tool to check the document layout before hitting 'print'.

Stop and think before printing something.

212. Reduce the number of printers

How many printers do you have in your building? Do you absolutely need them all? Would it really kill your staff to walk down a flight of stairs when they wanted to print something? How much money would it save your charity? Would it make them think twice about printing unnecessarily?

Why not remove a quarter of the printers in your organisation, and sell them to raise cash?

213. Save up external print jobs

Everyone knows that it is more cost-effective to buy print in bulk, but not many organisations actually do anything about it. We tend to order business cards as soon as

...it is more cost-effective to buy print in bulk...

people join, print direct mail once a month, and order posters as and when the need arises.

You can save a fortune on your print budget by simply planning ahead. Spend a few hours this week working out what print you will need over the next six months. See what you can order feasibly in advance and what you can hold back, so that you make one big order now and another in six months' time.

214. Reduce the paper weight that you buy from print firms

Downgrade the paper you use from 90gsm to 80gsm...

In tip 155 we looked at how you can save money by buying cheaper paper. Bear in mind that you can also save money by selecting cheaper paper options when ordering from professional printers. Whether it is a letterhead, brochure or some other pre-printed item you can easily save 10 per cent on your costs by downgrading the paper you use from 90gsm to 80gsm.

215. Print on both sides

Change default settings on all the printers in your office so that they always print on both sides. You will reduce your expenditure on both paper and ink while reducing your carbon footprint.

216. Print in black and white

...whenever you see an internal document in colour, question whether it could have been done in black and white...

It is nearly 50 per cent cheaper to print a document in black and white, so whenever you see an internal document in colour, question whether it could have been done in black and white, and encourage other managers to do the same. No one needs to make a big deal of it – simply point out that it would have been just as useful in black and white, and how much cheaper it is.

Before long, you will build a culture where people print in black and white unless there is a genuine need for colour.

217. Use your printer's software

Most printers come with software that allows you to control how it works. You can make some impressive savings by getting to know this software and using the tools on offer.

For example, by setting all your printers to draft mode you will use less ink immediately. There might be a slight reduction in print quality, but it is only really noticeable with large-scale colour documents. In fact, you might find that you are already using draft mode and are not aware of it.

Another setting which can be really useful is the 'fit to page' mode. This condenses content so that it all fits on to a single sheet of A4 paper. You might find a setting for this on your printer software, but you may find it also in the software that you are using. For example, in the Firefox web browser you will find a 'shrink to fit' mode in the print preview area.

218. Use a local printing firm

Transport accounts for a significant part of any print job. By using a local print firm you can reduce harmful emissions, support local businesses and cut your costs. Of course, you first need to make sure that they are up to the job.

219. Look into print management firms

Print management firms buy large quantities of print on behalf of several companies. They are often able to get good prices – partly due to their economies of scale, and

... by setting all your printers to draft mode you will use less ink immediately.

Often, print management firms are able to get good prices ...

119

partly because they are experienced print buyers who know all the techniques for getting the best value from a particular job.

They will know the best weight, size and quality for every item, and will ensure that you get exactly what you need for no more than you need to pay. You do have to pay them for providing this service, but if you are able to find a good one it can cut your print costs dramatically.

Chapter 17

Travel

220. Cut out unnecessary work-related travel

Work-related travel is not only very expensive, it is also highly damaging to the environment. This should be one area where you can make significant inroads into your costs, and where you should meet very little resistance from staff.

Take a look at your diary now. Look at all the meetings you have booked in. How many of them are really necessary? What would you save on travel and accommodation if you cancelled the unnecessary ones? What could you get done with the time you save?

Some meetings are very useful, but all too often meetings take place for no better reason than that they have always done so. Cancel them now, encourage your staff to do the same, and make an immediate saving.

... often meetings take place for no better reason than that they have always done so.

221. Hold more meetings at your premises

One quick and simple way to save money on work-related travel is to schedule more meetings at your premises. Look at your diary now. Is there one meeting that always seems to take place at the other person's place? Next time you arrange to meet them, suggest a change of venue. Encourage your colleagues to do the same.

222. Use online conferencing rather than travelling to meetings

Cartrefi Cymru is a charity that helps people with learning disabilities. Its staff are located throughout Wales, which for its managers has meant always a great deal of travelling to and from meetings. This was expensive and tiresome but they needed to confer, so it was inevitable.

However, with the introduction of online conferencing, all that has changed. Cartrefi Cymrus commissioned an online conferencing provider to install the equipment, train their staff and provide a helpdesk, and their staff now use the facilities every day. The management team is expected to save more than 100,000 miles of travelling each year, returning around 400 days of ineffective travel time. This is expected to save the charity around £50,000 a year in direct travel and hotel costs.

223. Plan ahead to avoid peak-time travel

Travelling at peak times is much more expensive than travelling at other times. For example, travelling on trains or planes on Friday is almost always more expensive than travelling on any other day of the week. This is simply because that is when the carriers experience the largest demand. Similarly, train travel costs more before 10am and between 5pm and 7pm.

Plan ahead to reduce your exposure to higher fares.

Plan ahead to reduce your exposure to these higher fares. Avoid site visits on Fridays, and schedule meetings for lunchtime rather than first or last thing in the day.

224. Buy train tickets 12 weeks early

Train travel can be incredibly cheap, or incredibly expensive – it all depends on how you buy it. Introducing an intelligent purchasing process for train travel could save your organisation thousands of pounds every year. For example, very often buying two singles works out cheaper than buying a return fare.

Most of us know that booking early is cheaper. However, not many people know that almost all advance fares are released exactly 12 weeks early. So get in there the minute they are released, and grab a bargain fare. You can even sign up at: www.thetrainline.com to receive alert emails the minute tickets for a particular journey go on sale.

Introducing an intelligent purchasing process for train travel saves thousands of pounds...

225. Always call to check for cheap train fares

Even if you cannot plan your journey that far in advance, you should always call – even if you are on your way to station – to see if any advance fares are available. Avoid using the 08457 484950 National Rail Enquiries number. Instead, use 0121 634 2040 and choose option 1. It costs less and you speak to exactly the same call centre.

226. Use season tickets for train travel

If you or your staff make a regular journey – say, to visit a project every week – it may be worth investing in a season ticket.

Try the season ticket calculator at: www.nationalrail. co.uk.

227. Look for special train deals

Frequently there are special deals out there if you know where to find them. Journeys such as Manchester to London can be made for as little as £1 each way. Check the website of your local travel operator and sign up for email updates, which can alert you to some great offers. Check these sites to find current deals: www.thetrain

...sign up for email updates, which can alert you to some great offers.

line.com, www.nationalrail.co.uk, www.nationalexpress .com and www.raileasy.co.uk.

228. Get refunds for train delays

If a train is more than half an hour late, you probably are entitled to a refund. Make sure that all your staff know this, and that they keep their tickets and pick up a form from the station.

229. Fly economy class

...you can easily save your charity several hundred pounds by spending a few hours in economy.

Just because you are flying on business, it doesn't mean that you have to fly business class. If you are on a long-haul flight, say to a conference in South-East Asia and you need to be on top form when you arrive, there might be a case for flying business class. However, for journeys within Europe, or for those where you have a day or two to recover, you can save your charity several hundred pounds by spending a few hours in economy.

If you already fly economy, as many in the voluntary sector do, why not look into charter flights? These can be even cheaper than economy-class scheduled flights.

230. Use budget airlines

Introduce a policy to favour budget airlines...

Why is it that when we book our holidays we immediately go online to find the cheapest fares that easyJet or Ryanair have on offer, but when we are flying abroad for business we automatically call British Airways or some other premium carrier? Introduce a policy to favour budget airlines and you could see your expenditure on air travel tumble quickly.

'Screenscrapers' trawl all the budget airlines' websites to find you the best possible deal. Popular ones include www.kayak.co.uk, www.skyscanner.net and www.travel supermarket.com.

231. Two return flights are sometimes cheaper than one

Airlines use sophisticated computer algorithms to price their tickets based on predicted demand. These sometimes throw up bizarre results, meaning that it can be cheaper to buy two return tickets and only use half of each – a process called back-to-back ticketing. Get into the habit of investigating all your ticket options rather than just paying for whatever you are offered first.

...it can be cheaper to buy two return tickets and only use half of each...

232. Use insurance brokers

Deal with an insurance broker rather than an insurance company. They are much better placed to negotiate a good deal and in most cases they will reduce your policy payments while increasing cover. The best place to start looking for one is the website of the British Insurance Brokers' Association (www.biba.org.uk).

Always ask a broker whether or not they receive a commission from the providers of any products they recommend. In terms of payment for this service: you should never have to pay the broker directly as they get paid by the insurance company. There are a number of good brokers that mostly deal with charity clients. One example is FirstCity (www.firstcity.com).

233. Encourage car sharing

Rather than employees driving separately to meetings and then submitting individual claims for petrol use, encourage them to share a car. Even if they are travelling from home rather than the office, it ought to

...encourage employees to share a car.

be possible for one to pick the other up. It might take a little organising, but if it can halve your car travel costs, it is worth it.

234. Stamp out wastage on taxis

With a bit of advance planning it can be easy to reduce the amount that you and your staff spend on taxis. Very often, because we know that we can just get a taxi if we are running late, we leave things until the last minute. If you and your team are incurable taxi users then consider setting up an account with a firm such as Addison Lee. This is always cheaper than hailing black cabs, and if you can negotiate a discount, in the long run it will work a fair bit cheaper even than local minicabs.

235. Avoid overnight stays

If you or your staff are travelling for work, do all you can to avoid overnight stays, simply because hotels are expensive. Try to schedule meetings so that staff can travel out and back in a day.

236. Use the Internet to find last-minute hotel offers

...look online to find a discounted last-minute room...

Every night across the world there are millions of hotel rooms sitting there empty. This costs the hotel owners billions of pounds, and they are always keen to sell this unused space – often at excellent rates. You could wait until the last minute, walk into a hotel and ask if they have any space for that night. You might get a very good deal. On the other hand, you might end up trawling the area for an entire evening, or sleeping in your car. Far better to look online at a site such as www.laterooms.com, which will find you a discounted last-minute room without the legwork.

237. Use budget hotels

Budget hotels used to mean uncomfortable rooms in inconvenient locations, usually right next to a motorway, and a surefire way to avoid a good night's sleep. However, things have changed. If your staff need to stay in hotels a lot then you may be able to cut costs by encouraging them to stay in one of the new range of clean, convenient and comfortable budget hotels that are now on the market.

... stay in one of the new range of clean, convenient and comfortable budget hotels ...

Maybe people always have stayed in more prestigious hotels while on business travel – if so, you could be cutting this budget by around 75 per cent. Most business travellers waste money on hotel facilities that they never need. Be honest: how often do you use the pool, gym, spa, concierge, meeting rooms and so on?

Chains such as Holiday Inn Express, Travelodge and Jurys Inn now offer clean, comfortable, basic accommodation in city centre hotels, often for less than £80 a night, and sometimes for considerably less. City Inn does not describe itself as a budget hotel, but it offers excellent value for under £100 a night in London, Glasgow, Manchester, Birmingham and Bristol.

238. Get staff to share hotel rooms

While most of us would prefer to have our own hotel room while travelling for work, these costs can mount up rapidly. A simple way of roughly halving the cost of hotel accommodation is to suggest that staff of the same gender share twin rooms.

239. Book apartments rather than hotel rooms

While the headline price of a serviced apartment might look higher than a hotel room, it actually may work out

A serviced apartment also provides space for meetings.

cheaper. This is partly because the person staying there can cook rather than spending money on restaurant meals or room service. It also provides space for meetings without the need to pay for additional rooms.

240. Consider staying in university halls of residence

If you are travelling to a meeting in a different part of the country and are facing a large hotel bill, look into what the local university can offer you. During the holidays, many offer their halls of residence as extremely good value accommodation, usually in well-located and peaceful spots. Prices can be as low as £22 per person. (See: www.budgetstayuk.com.)

241. Stay with family and friends

An excellent way to cut accommodation costs is to encourage staff to stay with friends and family when they travel for work. Many will be happy to do this, preferring home comforts to the faceless charms of a hotel room. However, you can provide a further incentive by offering a payment of say £25 for each night that they do this rather than staying in a hotel room. You save on accommodation costs, and they can put the £25 towards taking their hosts out for dinner to thank them for putting them up!

242. Cut meal costs

The cost of food that your staff eat while on the road might not be an enormous drain on your finances, and you might make yourself extremely unpopular if you try to impose a limit on the price of a meal, but every little counts. You might want to remind staff why it is so important that the organisation controls every cost, and suggest a reasonable amount for a meal while travelling.

243. Don't ignore travel agents

Travel agents charge a commission, and often are tied to promoting the travel and accommodation options of just one or two providers. However that does not mean that booking independently, through the Internet or the phone, is always cheaper.

In return for limiting the number of providers that they promote to just one or two, travel agents can receive special deals. So before you hit the buy button on what looks like an unbeatable work trip, pick up the phone to one or two business travel agents and just check whether in fact they can beat the price.

244. Don't pay for the expensive extras

Travel companies are notorious for offering a low-headline rate and then tacking on expensive little extras. Be wise to it, and make sure your staff are too. Don't go over your luggage weight allowance, and remove unnecessary insurance policies from tickets. Pennies soon add up to pounds.

... remind staff why it is so important that the organisation controls every cost ...

... travel agents can receive special deals.

Chapter 18

Fundraising

245. Concentrate on your most effective fundraising technique

Fundraising is essential for most charities. Most charities have to invest large amounts of money on attracting, retaining and energising donors. These might be individuals, they might be companies, or they might be government departments, but whoever they are, their funding is absolutely essential to the future of your organisation.

...be very wary of cutting back on your fundraising.

For that reason you should be very wary of cutting back on your fundraising. All too often, charity managers see financial problems on the horizon and take an axe to the fundraising budget. While this might trim costs in the short term, in the longer term it also cuts income.

However, this does not mean that you can't make your investment in fundraising work harder, or that you can't become more efficient in your fundraising, using innovative techniques and creative ideas to raise more funds with fewer resources.

Your first step must be to concentrate on your most effective fundraising technique. If you get a good chunk of your income from legacies without making much effort in that area, surely it makes sense to invest more resources there. If direct mail works well for you, why not do more of it? Whether it's telephone fundraising or street collections, focus your budget on what you do well.

246. Get accurate metrics on fundraising effectiveness

What is your most effective fundraising technique? Most charities think they know – but are you sure? The only way to be absolutely certain is to get accurate metrics. For every technique that you use, for every campaign that you run, you need to measure how much you spend on it, how many new donors it produces, and what value of income you receive.

It sounds far simpler than it actually is. To give just a few of the variables that you should consider: when working out costs, you need to factor in the time spent on the activity as well as the direct costs. When you work out how many donors a campaign has attracted, you should differentiate between one-off donors and regular Direct Debit donors. You also need to bear in mind that a one-off giver can be a major donation or a legacy donation. Equally, when you work out the return from a campaign, you need to bear in mind that a donation received today actually may have resulted from a campaign that the donor remembered from five years ago.

Metrics are not simple. As you look into it, you will discover far more complications than the examples given here. However, start off with a fairly basic model – how much you spent on an activity, how many new donors it produced and what value of donations you received – and evolve it over time. Before too long, you should have a fairly sophisticated system which allows you to allocate your fundraising budget efficiently.

...for every campaign that you run, measure how much you spend on it, how many new donors it produces, and what value of income you receive.

247. Cut out your least effective fundraising technique

Like most charities, you probably use a wide range of fundraising techniques: direct mail, street collections, legacies, government grants, and so on. If you need to make cutbacks, quite rightly you will be reluctant to reduce your fundraising activity – cutting fundraising is a surefire way to strangle your organisation slowly.

However, if the money simply is not there right now to pay for all your fundraising activities, you need to make a difficult decision.

... rank everything you do, so you can see which activities are good investments and which are less so.

In fact, that decision is relatively straightforward. You need to review your activities, and calculate how much each activity brings in and how much it costs. Remember to factor in staff time. This should allow you to rank everything you do, so you can see quite clearly which activities are good investments and which are less so. Then, cut out the activity that produces the poorest return.

248. Make everyone a fundraiser

You probably have a fundraising department. Your fundraisers will have a pretty clear-cut remit: to raise funds for the organisation. However, if they are to do that as cost-effectively as possible, they need the support of everyone in the organisation. Make it clear to everyone who works for your charity that they also have a responsibility to find new donors, pitch in with fundraising activities, and support the fundraisers wherever possible.

... run a monthly competition for the person who brings in the most funds.

This focus should extend all the way up the organisation, so that CEOs and senior managers are doing their bit to speak to major and corporate donors. By mobilising these resources, you will save yourself thousands of pounds on fundraising materials and consultants.

A good way to create a fundraising culture is to run a monthly competition for the person (outside of the fundraising department) who brings in the most funds. Award a small prize each month – it will focus minds on the importance of everyone acting as a fundraiser.

249. Use your trustees

Too many charity managers see their trustees as a burden, or an obstacle to be overcome at quarterly board meetings, but in fact they are a potentially invaluable resource. They are probably fairly experienced and senior people, with a large number of contacts in high places.

So, use these contacts. Ask your trustees if they can find people or businesses who will donate money, time or equipment. One phone call from a well-placed trustee can save you thousands of pounds and weeks of time in fruitless fundraising activity.

Ask your trustees if they can find people or businesses who will donate money, time or equipment.

250. Fundraise through your volunteers

If you don't use your volunteers for fundraising already, you are wasting one of your greatest resources. Start by canvassing their enthusiasm for doing this. You are likely to find that once asked, they are more than willing to help out in this way.

You will find also that they bring with them a network of contacts, many of whom can help with your fundraising. Maybe someone knows a public relations (PR) specialist, or someone who is good at speaking at events, or the head of philanthropy at a multinational corporation. Find out who is in their network, build a database, and start using this free resource to its full effect.

...your volunteers bring with them a network of contacts...

251. Target companies for donations

Most companies – especially larger corporates – want to be socially responsible. They have entire departments committed to ensuring that the business is environmentally friendly, a good and fair employer, open and honest in its shareholder reporting, and suitably philanthropic.

... the corporate world is a potentially rich seam of funding for your organisation.

Some argue that this is all a PR stunt, and that these companies only want to be *seen* to be giving back to society. From your point of view, however, whether this is the case is not especially important. What is important is that the corporate world is a potentially rich seam of funding for your organisation.

You can invest thousands of pounds in your fundraising efforts to individuals, sending mailer after mailer, building ingenious websites and devising brilliant publicity drives, and you will receive funds in return from your investment. Or you can make just as much money for your charity with just one well-judged approach to a corporate giving department.

However, fundraising in this area requires a particular approach and special skills. Various organisations run training in developing corporate support. This shows charities how to build relationships with these potentially very valuable corporate partners. These include the Directory of Social Change (www.dsc.org.uk) and the Institute of Fundraising (www.institute-of-fundraising. org.uk).

252. Stay up to date on corporate developments

... a business that is relocating could be willing to donate old furniture and equipment.

Just by reading the business pages of your daily newspaper or specialist business websites, you will be able to get an inside track on what is happening in the corporate world. You might read about a business that is relocating and which could be willing to donate old furniture and equipment. Or you might read about a company that could do with a boost to its public image through supporting your charity. Spending a few minutes every day keeping up to date with these developments could save your organisation thousands of pounds.

253. Become someone's 'charity of the year'

Rather than making small donations to many charities, many businesses prefer to nominate a charity of the year, with which they work for 12 months. This is highly beneficial for the charity as it means they have an almost guaranteed source of income for the year. It also can be a very useful partnership for raising the profiles of both organisations.

Cut the time and money that you need to invest in corporate fundraising by trying to become a charity of the year. If you already have corproate donors, ask them if they would consider this type of arrangement. Remember to explain how it would benefit them: less time spent on philanthropy decisions, close association with your cause, and so on.

254. Don't over-service major donors

While some major donors like to receive the recognition and personal service that comes with their own contact at the charity, others prefer to give their money quietly. Rather than assuming that everyone wants high levels of service, ask them what they want from you. Once you find out which major donors prefer to be left alone, you can transfer resources to those who like the attention. Or you can simply cut your costs in this area.

. . . ask your donors what they want from you.

255. Concentrate on lapsed donors

Someone who used to give money to your charity is much more likely to do so now than someone who has never done so. It makes sense to concentrate your fundraising efforts on that part of your database.

It is very rare that once someone has begun to give to a charity, they decide they no longer care...

Contact them to tell them about recent developments at the charity, and ask them to begin giving again. Often, their donations will have lapsed through negligence rather than intention. Or they will found themselves unable to give for some time but are now able to do so. It is very rare that once someone has begun to give to a charity, they decide they no longer care about the issue.

However, do know where to draw the line. At some point it will become more economical to target fresh leads than to keep going back to the same lists of lapsed donors.

256. Call your donors up

Rather than continuing to send your donors costly direct mail packs, why not just pick up the phone to them? It might take a bit more time, but it will be more effective. People are more likely to respond positively to a well-put and sensitively timed phone call than they are to yet another mailer.

People are more likely to respond positively to a well-put and sensitively timed phone call...

It should enable you also to refine your mailing lists, removing people who tell you that they are just not interested, and it will be a great deal cheaper than writing, designing, printing and posting out a mail pack.

It is unlikely that you and your team will have enough time to call everyone on your mailing list, but why not tackle 10 per cent of it, or even 2 per cent? If nothing else, it will trim 2 per cent off the cost of your next mailer.

257. See every point of contact as a fundraising opportunity

Spend less on dedicated fundraising materials by seeing every point of interaction with stakeholders as a potential fundraising opportunity. Do you send your donors, volunteers, trustees and employees an annual report? Then why not include a fundraising request with it? Don't limit yourself to posted material either – use your website, email signature and any face-to-face contact to remind stakeholders that you welcome any donations they can make.

258. Offer donors choice

Some donors like to hear from you once a month to be updated on exactly what you are doing with their money. Others would much rather you spent your time and money focusing on your charitable mission. Neither are wrong: both are entirely reasonable and valid opinons. However, if you persist in sending monthly updates to the latter type of donor, not only do you risk alienating them, but you are wasting valuable resources.

Ask all your current donors how often they would like you to communicate with them and through what medium. Then give them exactly that. Also, establish a system for asking all future new donors the same question.

... remind stakeholders that you welcome any donations they can make.

259. Don't just ask for money

A recent survey of 1,000 UK adults found that charities might have more success with fundraising by doing more, rather than asking for money. The research, commissioned by marketing company DMS, found that 39 per cent of respondents would use options such as buying charitable goods or raffle tickets rather than simply making donations.

This reluctance to part with money might be more pronounced during a recession, but even in the good times, charities can make the most of their fundraising investment by mixing cash appeals with raffles, requests for goods, and so on. Make sure you are not wasting money by repeatedly asking for cash from donors who

... charities might have more success with fundraising by doing more, rather than asking for money.

have made it clear already that they do not want to give cash.

260. Don't let bogus collectors steal your donations

According to Clothes Aid, a company which carries out doorstep collections for not-for-profit organisations, thefts of bags of clothing intended for charities increased by 30 per cent in the second half of 2008. This meant that charities were losing out on about 200 bags of clothing every week – a total of around £3 million per year.

If you suffer from this problem, take action. Make donors aware of it, and introduce ID cards for genuine collectors. Talk to your local police about ways of minimising the problem. You might be surprised at how much you can achieve. Clothes Aid reported a 30 per cent drop in thefts last year following an awareness campaign run in partnership with the police.

261. Get cheap deals on advertising

You might need to advertise – to raise awareness of your charity, to raise funds for a specific campaign, or for some other reason. If you have ever done this in the past, you will know that advertising is not cheap. Even small advertisements in relatively niche titles can cost thousands of pounds. At the other end of scale, full-page advertisements in Sunday supplements are beyond the budgets of all but the largest charities.

... cut your costs by booking your advertisements at the last minute.

However, you can cut your costs in this area by booking your advertisements at the last minute. Print publications have to fill a certain number of pages with advertising, and as print day draws nearer, advertising sales executives become ever more desperate to sell the space – at any price. This is not only the case with print advertising. If your budget stretches to radio or television, you should find that you are able to negotiate good deals with those media as well.

You even could consider letting them know what you can afford, and telling them that they can call you when they are ready to sell at that price. It might not happen every time, but you almost certainly will get yourself the occasional bargain.

262. Outsource specialist fundraising tasks

Most charities have the in-house capacity to produce direct mail literature, to organise a street collection, and to keep in contact with existing donors. However, few are able to do more technical, specialised tasks such as face-to-face Direct Debit sign-ups, mass telephone fundraising, database maintenance, and so on. Yet these are all ways in which fundraising can be made considerably more effective.

. . . face-to-face Direct Debit sign-ups, mass telephone fundraising and database maintenance can all make fundraising more effective.

You should certainly consider introducing them, but be wary of investing heavily in in-house resource. Instead, go to the experts. Speak to a few specialist consultants, and set up a short pilot with one of them. If it doesn't work, you should not lose too much money, and if it does, you will have discovered an entirely new revenue stream for your organisation. If the approach is particularly effective, over time you can build up your internal resource.

263. 'Piggyback' the mailings of local businesses

Ask local businesses if you can include your fundraising appeals in their mailings. They will be able to help a charity at no cost, and you will not have to pay for postage.

264. Use a mobile marketing service

...text messages can be a great way to reach donors.

At the time of writing, text donations to voluntary organisations were worth £6 million per year, and a growing number of charities were discovering that text messages can be a great way to reach donors. Research by nfpSynergy in late 2008 among more than 1,000 people aged 16–34 revealed that around one-third of respondents would be willing to donate to charity through SMS. However, because of excessive fees, VAT and other taxes, charities only receive 55p from each pound donated through this medium.

The Institute of Fundraising points charities to Luup mobile donations. These enable anyone over the age of 14 to pay, send and receive money by SMS, WAP, online or by phone to charity. Charities simply fill in a registration form and can start to accept donations immediately. There are no upfront fees, and Luup only receives a fee when the charity in question receives a donation. At the time of writing, Luup charged 2.5 per cent + 18p for transactions above £1.50.

Luup donations can be made spontaneously, can be made anytime anywhere, are secure and easy to use, cover any amount between 1p and £800, and are received immediately by the charity.

265. Stop putting pens in your mailings

When charities began putting pens in their mailings it was a very good idea. Many charities – notably Amnesty International, in the 1990s – used it to great effect. However, that was a long time ago. Now most people see them as a nuisance, and a growing number of people are concerned about the environmental impact of all this plastic going into the production of disposable pens. If you still include pens in your mailings, save yourself money and simply stop it.

266. Know how to get money from the government

There are millions and millions of pounds available as government funding for organisations just like yours. However, getting hold of it can be a time-consuming and costly exercise. Stop wasting time and money, and learn how to do it properly.

Invest in a short training course that will help you to understand the system, be aware of recent changes to the funding relationship between statutory and voluntary organisations, and know how to make bids in the appropriate language and style for statutory bodies.

267. Read the small print on grant applications

According to the Directory of Social Change, 48 per cent of all applications for central government grant programmes are ineligible at the first assessment stage. This is not to say that they were bad applications, simply that they are not eligible.

For example, organisations based in Wales apply for funds only available to English organisations. Non-charitable groups apply for funds only accessible to registered charities. Charities apply for £100,000 to funds which have a clear limit of £20,000 per application.

Funding application processes can be complicated. This is why the DSC publishes 27 funding guides and directories designed to make it easier for charities to find out who to apply to, and how to apply to them (see: www.dsc.org.uk).

... if you still include pens in your mailings, simply stop it.

... know how to make bids in the appropriate language and style for statutory bodies.

141

Read the small print before beginning your application…

Nevertheless, however complex these procedures are, there is no excuse for wasting charity resources by applying for grants that you simply have no chance of receiving. Read the small print before beginning your application, make absolutely certain that you are eligible, and only then start spending time and money on the process.

268. Understand full cost recovery

If you are involved in delivering any projects using public funds you should be aware of the phrase 'full cost recovery'. This is about making sure that you budget effectively so that your funding matches your expenditure. It sounds simple, but can be very tricky to get right. Full cost recovery can become a significant financial black hole for many charitable organisations.

Full cost recovery can become a significant financial black hole…

Invest in some training on full cost recovery. This will teach you about the importance of full cost recovery, the principles and methods involved in cost allocation and, crucially, how to prepare budgets, involving cost allocation, to arrive at the full cost of any project or activity.

269. Get a free fundraising healthcheck

How effective is your fundraising? Where you could you improve? How could you get a better return for the investment that you make? These are all questions that charity fundraisers and managers continuously ask themselves. The problem is that the best people to answer these questions – impartial fundraising experts – charge a lot of money to run these healthchecks.

So, you should jump at Fundraising Healthcheck – a free confidential fundraising healthcheck from the Institute of Fundraising and Think Consulting Solutions. The online diagnostic tool (available at: www.fundraisinghealth

check.org) provides a picture of a charity's fundraising practice as well as recommendations for developing fundraising programmes and investment strategies. You don't have to give the name of your charity, and the tool will not store or access any information about you.

Lindsay Boswell, chief executive of the Institute of Fundraising, said:

> It is more important than ever that charities assess the fundraising security of their organisations; that they look at their fundraising and determine whether it is the right mix in the intensity needed to achieve its goals. Fundraising Healthcheck is expected to provide maximum benefit for small to medium-sized charities that do not have a corporate business infrastructure or previous recession experience to draw from.

...It is more important than ever that charities assess the fundraising security of their organisations...

270. Monitor fundraising effectiveness more frequently

As the UK economy entered recession in 2009, most charities reviewed their finances and planned a response. The British Red Cross identified three main areas to focus on: improving monitoring, forecasting and reporting – particularly cashflow and head count.

Rohan Hewavisenti, the charity's director of finance and business development, has explained that the British Red Cross is reviewing and revisiting major items of expenditure in light of the latest finances. While it would continue to invest in fundraising during these difficult economic times, it would monitor the metrics even more closely than in the past. Hewavisenti said that he would be looking at them every week rather than every month.

The more frequently you can look at your fundraising metrics, the more likely it is that your investment will produce a good return.

The more frequently you can look at your own fundraising metrics, the more likely it is that your investment in that area consistently will produce a good return.

271. Focus your message

Focus your message clearly, and cut your media spend...

If your fundraising message is vague or poorly targeted, you will not be getting the maximum return possible from your investment. In other words, you could get the same result from fewer advertisements, fewer direct mail pieces, or whatever medium you are using. Focus your message more clearly, and either keep your media spend the same for a better return, or cut your media spend to get the same result.

Can you answer yes to every one of the following questions?

- Do you know exactly who is receiving your fundraising messages?
- Do you know what aspect of them resonates with that audience?
- Do they contain a clear call to action?
- Do they provide facts?
- Are those facts related to something meaningful to the audience?
- Are they as brief as they could be?

If not, you almost certainly can improve them.

Chapter 19

PR and newsletters

272. Invest time in building a PR strategy

PR is probably the most cost-effective way for a charity to promote itself. Done correctly, it is free advertising. In fact, it is more powerful than advertising, because you are not just paying for space in which you sell yourself, you are persuading an impartial and respected third party – a journalist – to do it.

PR is more powerful than advertising...

You can spend thousands of pounds on PR consultants, but if you lack the budget to do that, you should be able to build your own PR campaign fairly easily.

The first step is to get to know your media. You know who you want to reach, so which titles, channels or websites do they read, listen to and watch? Then, who are the key journalists at each one? Use the Internet and the phone to get the names, phone numbers and email addresses of those journalists. Bear in mind that journalists rely on people such as you contacting them with news stories and ideas for articles.

Send them an email to introduce yourself, your organisation, and the issues you want them to write about. If possible, arrange to meet up. However you do it, you need to find some way of getting them interested in your subject so that they write about it and come to you for information, opinion and soundbites.

273. Hire a press-release service

Keeping a media database up to date can be time-consuming, and writing press releases that get results is a skill that few people have. You almost certainly will get more coverage if you can hire professionals to keep your database and write your releases.

... writing press releases that get results is a skill that few people have.

Rather than taking on a full-time PR person, or hiring a full PR agency, many voluntary organisations prefer to use a press-release service. For a set fee (usually between £200 and £300), a professional writer will produce your press release and send it to an up-to-date list of relevant journalists. This is a relatively cost-effective way of disseminating your news through the media.

274. Write your own press releases

By far the cheapest option when it comes to press release writing is to do it yourself. It is a skill that can be learned like any other; you simply need to understand the principles involved, and put in a lot of practice. You need to be in it for the long term. Like advertising, PR does not work as a one-off.

... understand the principles involved, and put in a lot of practice.

To decide what to write about in your press releases, think about what will interest the readers of the publications that you plan to approach. Too many press releases focus solely on what the writer or organisation is doing. The readers of these publications probably are not very interested in what you or your charity is doing. They are more likely to be interested in what your news means for them. So, write about that instead.

Try to give as much specific detail as possible, keep the language clear and simple, avoid jargon, and double check for basic errors in spelling, grammar and facts. Send your press releases in the body of an email, with an enticing subject line that will encourage the journalist to open and read it. Then follow up with a phone call after a couple of days.

275. Get hold of editorial schedules

As well as sending press releases to keep your media targets informed of what you are doing and how it is relevant to their readers, remember also that those media have their own editorial calendars. These detail what subjects they will cover in which issue. Get hold of these schedules, work out how your messages can fit into those categories, and pitch your idea to the journalist who is writing the article. Get it right, and this can be a very straightforward and inexpensive way of getting your message out there.

... pitch your idea to the journalist who is writing the article.

276. Run a competition

If your press releases are not hitting the mark with journalists, and you cannot find any slots on the editorial schedule that fit in with what you want to talk about, running a competition can be a great way of setting the agenda. This is more expensive because you may need to provide a prize, but it is less expensive than advertising. If the competition is sufficiently interesting and the enticing, it can be much more effective than advertising.

... running a competition can be a great way of setting the agenda.

277. Hold a stunt

Another way of getting the media to notice you is to stage some kind of stunt. It can be anything from lying in a bath of beans to spending a night in the local police cells. The more outrageous it is, and the more conducive to a striking photograph or news report, the more likely it is that the media will use it. Just ensure that your stunt remains within the law, and that you can shift the coverage away from the stunt and on to the actual issues for which you want to get coverage.

278. Get out there and speak

Instead of spending hundreds or thousands of pounds producing marketing materials to reach a particular audience, why not find an event at which many of them will be, and offer yourself as a free speaker? Event organisers are always looking for good speakers, and this can be an excellent opportunity to convey your message to a relevant and captive audience. It also gives you the opportunity to speak to your prospects individually after your talk. Remember that if you impress, people will talk about you to people they know. You will have begun to create a buzz.

... if you impress, people will talk about you to people they know.

279. Get media training

Finding opportunities to promote your message through the media is hard work in itself. However, once you have found them, you still need to make the most of them. That is where media training comes in.

Delivered by experienced journalists and spokespeople, media training helps you to understand how the media operates, what journalists want from spokespeople, and how you can make sure that your message comes across loud and clear. It is invaluable in maximising the potential of the media. It is also startlingly expensive, with day-long courses usually costing upwards of £2,000.

... media training helps you to understand how you can make sure that your message comes across loud and clear.

However, cheaper options are available to charities. For example, CSV (www.csv.org.uk) runs courses staffed by volunteer journalists and spokespeople on topics such as public speaking, lobbying and copywriting. See also the wide range of courses offered by the Media Trust (www.themediatrust.co.uk).

280. Send newsletters by email

A newsletter is a great way of staying in touch with donors, partners and potential supporters. It also can be incredibly expensive to run; not only do you need to pay people to write, edit and design the content, you also have to print and mail it out. However, by shifting to email newsletters you can remove printing and mailing costs.

... by shifting to email newsletters you can remove printing and mailing costs.

Some observers believe that email newsletters are less effective than printed newsletters. They argue that no one reads them, and that they are too easy to delete. Yet printed newsletters are just as easy to ignore or to throw in the bin. This negative perception around email newsletters has gained ground simply because so few organisations produce good email newsletters. If you are able to produce effective email newsletters, you will save money and keep your stakeholders updated and engaged.

281. Include topics that interest the readers, not the writers

It can be tempting to see an email newsletter as an opportunity to hold forth on an exciting new appointment or a fresh initiative that you are running. No doubt these are very important to the people writing about them, but you need to bear in mind that your readers might not immediately grasp why they should be interested.

... put yourself in the shoes of the readers and think about what makes it interesting for those readers.

The person writing needs to put themselves in the shoes of the readers, and think thoroughly about the aspect of that new appointment or that fresh initiative that makes it interesting for those readers. What does it mean to them? Why should they want to read about it?

282. Write clearly

... keep sentences short, cut unnecessary words and avoid meaningless clichés and jargon.

Very often, people think that when they write for something 'official' such as an email newsletter they need to start producing long, convoluted sentences packed full of obscure words and padded out with meaningless qualifiers. This simply makes it difficult to follow, and puts readers off. Encourage the person writing to keep sentences short, cut unnecessary words, always use the most straightforward word available, and avoid meaningless clichés and jargon.

283. Make your newsletter format appealing

Ideally, all the important information should be above the fold, as many people will read the top part of the email and not bother to scroll down. Most practitioners agree that content looks far more appealing to the eye in HTML format. Break up the copy into readable chunks of between 300 and 800 words, interspersed with graphics.

284. Be clear about the sender and subject in your newsletters

Almost half (40–50 per cent) of people open an email based on who it is from ...

The name of the sender and the content in the subject line both have a major effect on whether or not an email is opened. Almost half (40–50 per cent) of people open an email based on who it is from, and 50–60 per cent do so based on the subject line. Make it clear that the email is from a charity they are involved with, and make the subject line enticing.

285. Be regular with your newsletters

A newsletter that is sent once every three months is not a newsletter. The content will be out of date and irrelevant. At the very least you need to send newsletters once a month, and probably once a week. You also need to send them at the same time, and on the same day, so that recipients get used to receiving them and reading them.

...you need to send newsletters once a month, and probably once a week.

286. Replace mailouts with email wherever possible

Abi Crawford is managing executive of the Multiple Sclerosis Resource Centre (MSRC). She says:

MSRC is a small national charity with just 11 staff, so cutting costs is always going to be key. We work hard to find ways to cut costs without compromising on providing a high level of care to anyone fundraising for the charity. One of the ways we have drastically cut our costs with fundraising events is effective use of email.

For instance, the Flora London Marathon is our biggest fundraising event of the year. We will raise around half of our annual income from this one event, and we usually have somewhere in the region of 130 runners. Three years ago we overhauled the whole way we interact with the team – instead of sending a costly eight-page, full-colour newsletter, which would take some time to put together, I started to send a monthly e-newsletter. This not only reduced print, postage and my time but it had the added benefit of keeping the runners much more engaged with the charity.

One of the ways we have drastically cut our costs with fundraising events is effective use of email.

However, that is not all, as Crawford explains:

We also stopped sending receipts for sponsorship received by post. We now send an email receipt unless the participant specifically needs a receipt on headed paper. We explained to the runners why we were changing to

151

this method, and not one person complained – they could see that it vastly reduced costs.

287. Build a culture of data cleanliness

...build and maintain a good database of recipients.

Whatever materials you are sending out, you need to build and maintain a good database of recipients. This is especially true for your direct mail work. Direct mail has been a key part of charity fundraising for many years now. It is an affordable method of reaching a large number of people with a specific message, and it is also very easy to measure its effectiveness. However, that effectiveness can be hampered by inaccurate data.

If you are sending mail to people who have moved or died, or no longer want to support you, you are not only wasting your charity's resources, but running the risk of severely damaging your charity's reputation. The same is true of data with inaccurate or incomplete addresses.

For this reason, you need to encourage your entire organisation to make data a top priority. If everyone recognises the cost of poor data, and sees it as part of their job to keep it clean, you will save yourself hundreds of pounds in wasted print, postage and processing.

288. Establish a system for keeping data clean

There are two ways of acquiring new donor data: you either buy it, or you acquire it yourself. If you buy it, make sure that it is from a reputable source. If you acquire it yourself, start by establishing a foolproof system for keeping it.

The key is to know what you have, and where you have it. Make sure that there is a system for staff to enter data, completing certain fields such as name, address, phone number and email address.

Then, don't ever relax about it. Data decays at a frighteningly rapid rate, and you need to stay constantly on top of this. For many organisations, it is cost-effective to pay a software bureau regularly to clean their data.

Data decays at a frighteningly rapid rate, and you need to stay constantly on top of it.

289. Obey the Data Protection Act

The Data Protection Act became law in 1998, and if you collect, store or use data in any way, it applies to you. Ignoring it puts you at risk of prosecution. Following it may help you to keep your data accurate and up to date.

Remember these four key points.

- If you gather data then you must gain consent to use it for a specific purpose, and then you must use it only for that purpose.
- If you do any electronic marketing, in some circumstances you must get explicit permission from potential recipients to include them on the mailing list. In other circumstances, for example when you have an existing relationship, you can include them on the list and provide a way that they can ask to be removed if they would like. For more information on this see www.ico.gov.uk/for_organisations/topic_specific_ guides/marketing.aspx.
- Don't keep data for longer than is necessary to fulfil the purpose for which it was collected.
- Don't allow any third parties to process data that you own until they agree to comply with your processing instructions – especially in relation to disclosure and security.

Don't keep data for longer than is necessary to fulfil the purpose for which it was collected.

290. Cut your data-cleaning costs with specialist software

The mental health charity Mind historically had used traditional bureau services to clean its data for fundraising mailings. However, by implementing a software solution called Cygnus Embedded Suppressions, it was able to save 50 per cent on these costs. In 2007, the charity launched 12 mailing campaigns, which generated a record return on investment, partly because the data was cleaned more efficiently and cost-effectively.

Mind's database manager, Yael Dion, said:

> *Cygnus has allowed us to be the ones responsible for how clean our data is and how effective our mailing activity is. We have cuts costs dramatically, enabling us to plough funds back into supporting the thousands of people who experience the effects of mental distress.*

Chapter 20

The Internet

291. Use the web to reach young people

The Internet can be a rich source of cost savings for your charity. War Child is one of many charities to recognise how the Internet can help to reduce its expenditure on travelling round the UK's schools and colleges. Traditionally, like many charities, it has recognised the importance of getting its message through to the next generation, and has invested time and money on this activity.

The Internet can be a rich source of cost savings for your charity.

However, the launch of its innovative social networking site Angry Mob (www.angrymob.org.uk) means that it can reach millions of young people without anyone having to go anywhere. Aimed at young people, the site is a place where children can learn about key global issues, express opinions about events around the world, and celebrate their achievements.

Angry Mob forms part of War Child's Citizenship classroom resources for the National Curriculum, funded by the Department for International Development, and is targeted at students in Years 9 to 11. The site provides a space for schools to promote active participation in school initiatives, encourage student involvement and mobilise them to action in support of War Child's cause. Angry Mob also enables users to post blogs, join in forum discussions and upload videos.

War Child worked with digital agency Enable Interactive on this project. Matt Connolly, the agency's strategy director, says:

Although War Child has a great profile, it is a small charity with limited funds and a huge vision. This was an incredibly ambitious project. However, with innovative thinking, use of smart technology and close collaboration with War Child's project team, we've been able to deliver the foundations for a fantastic online community.

292. Perform your own website audit

How good is your website? Does it raise awareness of your cause? Does it encourage donations? Is it easy to find and use? How could it be improved? Many organisations spend thousands of pounds on consultancies that will run detailed web audits and give them answers to these questions. However, you can save yourself that expense by running a simple and quick self-audit.

Visit your website, and look at it through the eyes of a first-time visitor.

Visit your website, and look at it through the eyes of a first-time visitor. Is it really as user-friendly as you think? Does it really convey the messages that you want?

You even could ask someone you know, who is unconnected to your charity, to do this mystery shopping for you. A fresh pair of eyes may produce unexpected insights.

293. Encourage users to create your online content

... the most successful websites are the ones that are regularly updated.

You probably know that the most successful websites are the ones that are updated regularly. Regular updating encourages users to come back for new content and to spend longer when they are there. However, you are probably equally well aware of how much time and money it can take to keep a website up to date.

Increasingly, charities are encouraging users to provide the content for their websites. Through free sites such as

Flickr and Youtube, people can post pictures and videos on your site. Not only does this save you money, it also engages your supporters, and provides visitors to your website with relevant content.

For example, in June 2007 CAFOD asked attendees at the World Can't Wait event in London to post their pictures and videos from the day on its site. For zero cost, its website was packed full of lively, up-to-date content that was directly relevant to visitors.

294. Use free analytical tools to optimise search

Ryan Scott is director of search at online marketing agency twentysix Search, and he has years of experience at helping charities use the Internet as a cost-effective way of marketing themselves.

He offers this advice:

One of the biggest mistakes charities make with online marketing is not knowing who their target audience is and adopting a "one size fits all" approach to communication. Free analytical tools such as Google Analytics or Yahoo's Index tools tell you who is visiting your website, whether they arrived via a search engine, what search terms they used to find you, what page they landed on, when and where they left, the peak times for visitors, and a whole host of other useful information that can help shape your communications programme and your website to work more efficiently.

These systems are simple to use, and they can be automated to run regular reports every day that can be deposited in your inbox. They also offer a dashboard to monitor other online marketing activity, such as Google Adwords activity, email campaigns and online advertising. These free tools can give a real insight into the problem areas of your online marketing campaigns and the areas that work well.

One of the biggest mistakes charities make is not knowing who their target audience is.

295. Make it easy to apply for jobs on your website

Given how expensive recruitment advertisements and agencies are, it is incredible how many voluntary organisations choose not to have a vacancies page on their website. What is more, a remarkable proportion of those that do put potential recruits off with tedious application forms that ask irrelevant questions.

... have a page on your website that advertises vacancies.

Cut your recruitment costs, and have a page on your website that advertises vacancies. Keep it frequently updated, make it simple for people to contact you, and make sure you respond to everyone in a timely fashion.

296. Use online networks to recruit

An increasingly common method of recruitment is to use online business networks such as LinkedIn (www.linkedin.com). It costs nothing to set up a profile. You then invite everyone you know to link to you, and to introduce you to the people they know. Before long, you have an extensive network of people to whom you can broadcast messages.

When you are recruiting next, simply send out the message on LinkedIn, asking those in your network if they know of anyone who fits a certain profile. More and more employers are doing this, spending just 10 minutes a day building a network and interacting with it, and many of them are finding it to be an inexpensive way of recruiting new staff.

For certain types of training, the Internet can offer the ideal solution.

297. Use online training

For certain types of training, the Internet can offer the ideal solution. Not only does it remove the need for staff to travel to a training venue, taking time away from work and incurring travel expenses, but they can learn at their own pace. In addition, it tends to be cheaper than classroom training.

However, don't make the mistake of believing that all your training can be done online. This approach works better for knowledge-based topics rather than skills-based ones, and it depends on a high level of commitment and motivation from the people doing the training. However, pick the participants and the subjects carefully, and you will be able to save a lot of money.

298. Set up self-service human resources

Much of the work done by the HR department involves maintaining records. It is straightforward but time-consuming. In fact, employees could do it themselves very easily, and generally they would prefer to do it themselves. This would allow them to see how much holiday time they have left, exactly how much they have been paid and why, and so on. There are a growing number of online applications that will allow you to do exactly this. They are not free, but they are generally cheaper than paying an HR professional to fill in forms.

299. Put expense claims online

Specialist expenses agency GlobalExpense believes that while 15 per cent of staff expense claims processed in-house should be rejected, only 1 per cent are actually thrown out. It argues that this lax in-house management of staff expenses is costing British firms more than £1 billion a year. The voluntary sector will account for a sizeable chunk of this.

... implement an online expenses system.

One possible solution is to implement an online expenses system. In these systems, staff log on to an external agency's website and fill in an online expenses form. Receipts are posted to the agency, which checks that claims are genuine before line managers approve them. Online validation reports accounting for every receipt are produced, so that managers have a clear view of who is spending what. Meanwhile, any changes to UK and European tax law are updated automatically on to the system.

300. Use online networking sites to raise funds

... look into using the many free networking sites now available.

The Internet can be a highly effective tool for raising funds, and you should look into using the many free networking sites now available. For example, BT Tradespace can provide you with a free online presence. You can interact with other members, raise your profile, use the free Paypal system to accept donations – in short, do everything that a website would allow you to do, but without the associated cost.

In the same way, if you already have a website, a 'Share on Facebook' button can be a great free way of using the viral nature of the Internet to disseminate a message to a large audience in a very short space of time. St John Ambulance uses this well, allowing visitors to its website to add First Aid information to its Facebook pages.

Meanwhile, Twitter is a social networking site that enables users to add very short updates of their activity. Other users can choose to view an individual's updates. Brands have been using the site to spread information about new products, new marketing campaigns, and so on. You could look into using it in this way. Why not join today, issue a few posts and see who signs up to find out more from you?

301. Run a blog

The term 'blog' comes from the phrase 'weblog'. A blog is essentially an online series of postings by an individual or organisation. It is an inexpensive way for you to spread your charity's messages online. Because readers are encouraged to comment on your blogs too, it is a great way to use the Internet to build engagement and dialogue with your stakeholders.

Setting up a blog is very easy. You can do it through a range of sites, such as Typepad (www.typepad.com) and Blogger (www.blogger.co.uk), for just a few pounds. Then you just start writing. There are more than 100 million blogs in the world, so you are competing in a crowded market. However, use the tips below and before you know it, you may have built a loyal following and found a very cheap new way of marketing your charity.

- Pick a topic that is likely to interest your target audience, but make sure it is one on which you have a lot to say.
- Post at least five times a week.
- Make your posts concise, lively and focused.
- Ensure that your spelling, grammar and facts are all correct.
- Encourage everyone you know to subscribe to it and leave comments.
- Read other charity blogs and leave comments there.

A blog is an inexpensive way for you to spread your charity's messages online.

161

Chapter 21

Consultants

302. Assess which is best: outsourcing, or working in-house

…it may be that you are better off outsourcing your finance function to a firm of accountants.

In some cases you will be able to save money by outsourcing an activity or function. For example, it may be that you don't have enough work for a full-time financial controller, and so you are better off outsourcing your finance function to a firm of accountants.

In other cases, it will make more sense to bring the function in-house. You might find that you are spending so much on fundraising agencies that you could cut costs by hiring a full-time fundraiser.

Whether an activity or function is performed more cost-effectively in-house or externally will depend on your organisation, your current circumstances, and the relative abilities of the staff and consultants available to you. It is important, though, that you consider your options in every department of your organisation. Look at each in turn and think about whether you could save money by outsourcing it or bringing it in-house. Consider costs carefully, and think about future requirements.

These are not decisions to make lightly, but neither are they decisions to shelve – you might find that you could be saving money for your organisation.

303. Bring in the experts

As your charity grows, you will find that you need to bring in more and more external consultants and agents.

Whether for finance, HR, the law, marketing, organisational development, strategy, quality management, technology or facilities management, there are thousands of consultants out there. If you pick the right person, set up the right deal and manage the relationship in the right way, they can do a huge amount to save money for your charity.

However, get all that wrong, and they will just cost you money. Many organisations are too afraid of getting it wrong to take the leap and use these experts. Don't fall into that trap – instead, learn how to get it right.

... the right person can do a huge amount to save money for your charity.

304. Know why you need external help

Too many relationships with consultants are doomed before they even have begun, simply because the person doing the buying lacks a clear idea of why they need a consultant in the first place. Your first stage must be to work out what exactly the problem is that the consultant will solve, or the benefit that they will bring. Never begin by deciding that you need a web designer to build you a new website. Decide first why you need a website, then why an external designer is the best person to deliver that.

Your first stage must be to work out what exactly the problem is that the consultant will solve...

305. Know what you need in a consultant

In the same way that any recruitment process should begin with a detailed job specification, so you need to spend some time scoping out what exactly you are looking for in a consultant. Is it essential that they have experience of working for charities, or would you value more highly the convenience of working with a consultant based just down the road? Whatever your criteria are, write them down, perhaps in three columns: must have, should have, and could have.

There are no rules about what makes a good or bad consultant – your requirements are unique to you – but you might want to consider the following two points before hiring any external supplier.

First, consultants are notorious for speaking a strange language known as 'management speak'. It has many varieties – IT consultants have their own language, legal specialists yet another – but what all of them have in common is the fact that, to the lay listener, they are largely incomprehensible. Many of them speak this language in an attempt to appear knowledgeable when they are not, and to baffle their clients into paying over-inflated fees.

Don't fall for it. If you cannot understand every single word they say, then ask them to explain themselves more clearly. If they are unable to do this, be very wary of hiring them.

...do not underestimate the importance of personal chemistry.

Second, do not underestimate the importance of personal chemistry. It matters that they have all the right qualifications, skills and experience – and these are, of course, very important attributes – but if you simply do not get on with someone, the relationship is very unlikely to work out.

306. Don't be put off by consultants' day rates

When comparing the cost of external consultants with the salaries of in-house staff, many charities are put off by the day rates that consultants charge. However, if you only need a £1,000-a-day consultant for 30 days a year, they are still cheaper than a full-time employee on £30,000 a year, once you have paid National Insurance and all the other costs associated with full-time employees. On top of this, bear in mind that if a consultant is charging £1,000 a day they should have much higher levels of expertise than anyone you would be able to hire for £30,000 a year.

307. Run a rigorous selection process

Once you know exactly why you need a consultant, have set aside a suitable budget and have pinned down exactly what you need in a consultant, you need to begin your selection process. If you are hiring a freelancer for a few days' work you may be able to put in a quick call, get an emailed quote, and set it all up without too much fuss. However, if you are spending more on an agency for a longer-term contract, you need to make absolutely certain that you pick the right one.

The first place you should start is with desk research. Try to find out who are the best suppliers in the area. Search the Internet. Look at magazines. Ask trade associations. Visit conferences. Ask other charities who they use. Some umbrella bodies such as NCVO (the National Council for Voluntary Organisations) and BOND (British Overseas NGOs for Development) run approved consultant schemes listing accredited providers with experience of working in the voluntary sector.

Once you have a list of potential suppliers, contact them to ask if they would like to be considered for the contract. Begin with an exploratory meeting at your premises. Tell them what you want to achieve. Don't grill them too much at this stage, this is an exploratory meeting to see if you have anything in common and can work together.

Begin with an exploratory meeting at your premises.

Then, arrange to visit their premises. If possible, drop in unannounced. You can find out much more than you might expect from things such as the décor, the expressions on people's faces as you walk around, the conversations you overhear while waiting in reception.

In the final meeting, they should put their proposal to you. Once you have chosen one you like, take up references. Even if you are entirely convinced that the supplier is ideal for you, always take up references.

308. Agree a mutually beneficial deal

You want to get the price down as far as possible, but be careful about going too far with this. In most cases you should not accept their first price, but don't drive too hard a bargain. Most consultants have a fairly flexible supply of labour: they will accept a much lower price to win any contract, but they will want to make it profitable. If the price is reduced, they will make simply a corresponding reduction in the amount of time that they spend working for you, and you will receive a sub-standard service.

Make sure that you know what you are buying. Ask the supplier to detail exactly what you will receive for the price you agree, and make sure that there are no unexpected extras, such as travel expenses, set-up charges, and so on.

309. Manage consultant relationships carefully

Getting the right consultant on the right deal might feel like the end of the project, but in reality it is only the beginning. You need to manage the relationship carefully, and this should begin with a clear project plan. Both parties need to agree deliverables, a timetable and a review procedure. You need to have a clear idea of the input you have to make into the project.

Managing these relationships takes time, so plan ahead for it. Allocate enough time, stick to the agreed dates for review meetings, and be constructive in these, evaluating progress honestly but looking ahead. Keep your consultant up to date on your priorities so that they can meet your needs. Finally, don't be too optimistic. Bear in mind that most projects get delayed; however long you think your project will take, build in some slack for these inevitable delays.

310. Review consultant relationships frequently

Review your consultant relationships regularly to ensure that the external advisers you have on board continue to provide you with the very best value. At least once a year, go through this process again. Think about whether you need a consultant at all and, if so, what you need in a consultant. Then check that your current provider is still offering exactly that, make sure you have a deal that is still working for both parties, and consider what you can do to improve the way that you manage the relationship.

...make sure you have a deal that is still working for both parties...

311. Learn from the experts, then do it yourself

Once you have selected the right consultants, agreed a good deal and the relationship is working well, it can be tempting to see the set-up as a permanent arrangement. You might change the supplier every once in a while, but whatever happens, that aspect of your work is always outsourced. However, this could be wasting you tens of thousands of pounds every year.

Once your staff have worked alongside an external expert for a few years, it is very likely that they will have a good idea of how to do the work themselves. If this does become the case, there is absolutely nothing to stop you ending a relationship with an expensive consultant and bringing the activity back in-house.

...there is absolutely nothing to stop you ending a relationship with an expensive consultant...

Don't feel guilty about it. Consultants expect their clients to do this – that is partly why their fees are higher. Your job is to save money for your charity, and by doing this you can wipe a significant amount from your overheads.

Before you take the plunge, make absolutely sure that your staff will be able to do the job as well as your consultants. The last thing you want to do is to have to go back to the

167

consultant in a few months' time and ask them to come back on board. Of course, they will be happy to help you again, but you may find that their fees have risen.

312. Use a cost-saving consultancy

One consultancy that you should definitely consider using if you are trying to save money is a cost-saving consultancy. The Charity Supply Company is one of several that specialise in the voluntary sector. It works solely for charities such as RNID, Romanian Orphanage Trust, the Refugee Council, Mencap, the Media Trust and the MS Society, helping them to procure goods at the best possible price.

The process is fairly straightforward. You tell the company what you need. It might be 10,000 annual reports, half a dozen computers, vehicles or whatever. Then you tell them the best price you have been able to find. It will find a quality company prepared to match the specification and beat the price, and you pay a commission of 30 per cent of the saving.

The Charity Supply Company claims to save charities an average of more than 25 per cent...

Cost-saving companies are able to find these savings because they know the best suppliers, how to buy cost-efficiently, and are able to negotiate good rates. The Charity Supply Company claims that it saves charities an average of more than 25 per cent, and it claims to have saved Mencap more than £3,000 on T-shirts, posters, leaflets, promotional fliers and so on for fundraising events, at an average discount of 30 per cent.

313. Use freelancers rather than agencies

With the advent of widespread broadband it has become easier than ever before for individuals to set themselves up in business, offering services that were only available previously from specialist agencies.

From web designers to legal advisers, accountants, human resource experts and copywriters, there are now thousands of these freelancers out there. Crucially for you, they can be an inexpensive alternative to those agencies. Often they work from home, so they have few overheads. Furthermore, you don't need to subsidise their managers' salaries or their sales and marketing efforts. You just pay for their services.

In the past, perhaps freelancers have had a bad reputation. They have been seen as people between jobs, or who have been rejected by serious employers. Increasingly, though, freelancing is a viable career option for people who have developed a level of expertise in their area of specialisation but prefer to remain practising it rather than move into management.

Very often, you will receive a better service from a freelancer than you will from an agency...

Very often, you will receive a better service from a freelancer than you will from an agency which has its top people in managerial or sales roles who will then pass you over to a fresh graduate for the day-to-day work. Look at every service you buy in, and do some research to see if you can find a freelancer who will do it more effectively for less money.

314. Hire 'no saving, no fee' consultants

If you are concerned that hiring cost-saving consultants might end up actually costing you money, look into hiring them on a 'no saving, no fee' basis. In most cases, they will charge simply a percentage of the saving that they make for you, so there is no risk to your organisation, and they have a strong incentive to save you money. This is what South London Nursing Homes did, to impressive effect. While it is a private nursing home rather than a charity, it has a story from which many charities can learn.

In most cases, cost-saving consultants will charge simply a percentage of the saving they make you...

South London Nursing Homes opened its first nursing home, The Pines, in Putney, west London, in the early 1980s. Its aim was (and still is) to provide a high-quality home for those requiring care. It has since opened Knowle Park in Cranleigh in 1986 and Galsworthy in Kingston in 1991. The nursing homes were brought together as South London Nursing Homes Ltd in 1996, and now care for a total of 164 residents.

Steve Carroll, Operations Manager for South London Nursing Homes, realised the importance of effective cost management, and had reviewed various expenses himself and found savings. Although pleased with his achievements, his work highlighted to him how time-consuming such reviews could be – particularly on top of all his other duties.

Bearing this in mind, Carroll met with some cost-saving consultants. He says:

Their no-saving, no-fee proposal was particularly attractive, as it minimised the risk to us if no savings were achieved and, if savings were found, it certainly made paying fees worthwhile.

The consultants quickly found savings of £4,770 in office supplies, £2,824 in laundry, £8,035 in janitorial supplies, and £4,727 in medical supplies. Jenkinson says:

We managed to negotiate savings with existing suppliers and also tendered to alternative suppliers for each service. In two areas these alternative suppliers offered greater savings without compromising service levels, and we were happy to change suppliers to achieve these higher savings.

The consultants also reviewed expenditure on insurance. They were able to achieve savings of £3,475. More importantly, their investigations uncovered the fact that the organisation's incumbent broker had understated the size of the operation. As a consequence, it was potentially underinsured. This issue was addressed, and South London Nursing Homes now has the correct level of cover at a lower price, while retaining the original broker.

Their no-saving, no-fee proposal was particularly attractive, as it minimised the risk to us if no savings were achieved...

Chapter 22
Legal issues

315. Stay out of court

Legal action is expensive. Not only do you have to pay for lawyers, but you have to spend hours of your time on the process. If you lose, you might have to pay your opponent's costs as well. So where possible, avoid it. Use arbitration and mediation services instead, try to agree a compromise that suits all parties, and save yourself a lot of sleepless nights.

316. Stay up to date with employment law

Employment law is far from the most exciting subject in the world, and staying up to date with it can be expensive. Training courses can cost hundreds of pounds and take you out of the office for days at a time. Hiring experts to advise you is hardly a cheaper solution.

However, failing to stay up to date with employment law is by far the most expensive option. As evidence for this, consider the sums awarded to staff who have been unfairly dismissed by charities. To take one example, in July 2008 Disability Action Yorkshire was ordered to pay the maximum compensation for unfair dismissal of £60,600 to its former chief executive. It defied the order, and in November 2008 was ordered to pay a further £15,000.

This was far from an isolated instance. In fact, such rulings and awards against charities are fairly common.

...failing to stay up to date with employment law is by far the most expensive option.

171

In another example, in November 2008, Turning Point Scotland was ordered to pay £22,000 compensation to a worker who had been sacked after firing a toy gun at work. The employee had been keen to develop new activities for clients after laser gun and paintball activities were dropped because of the cost, so he brought in a toy gun and demonstrated it to staff at a meeting. He was later accused of bringing an air weapon or imitation firearm to work, and was sacked for gross misconduct. The tribunal heard that in fact the gun was not an air weapon, and normally would not fall into any of the categories covered by the Firearms Act 1968.

Would you have known how to handle either of these situations? How would your organisation cope with having to pay out such a high sum to a former employee? When you consider how complex employment law can be, and when you realise the potential cost implications of a mistake, suddenly the cost of staying up to date with employment law seems a great deal more reasonable.

317. Get the best deal on employment law advice

The Government offers a wealth of free advice…

Employment law is not an area where you should cut corners, but equally it is not one where you need to waste money. There are some excellent sources of free information in this area. The Government offers a wealth of free advice on its website at: www.direct.gov.uk. HR industry publication *Personnel Today* runs a well-respected website with updates on current developments, at: www.personneltoday.com. Meanwhile, mediation service ACAS provides a free A–Z of employment law on its website at: www.acas.org.uk.

318. Get a good lawyer

A good lawyer will not be cheap. However, they should save you money by advising you early on of the correct course of action, steering you away from costly and damaging legal action.

Begin your search on a website such as the Law Society (www.lawsociety.org.uk) or Simple Free Law Adviser (www.sfla.co.uk), both of which hold databases of legal firms across the country.

Look for lawyers with experience of working with charities. Check with the Law Society how long the firm has been operating, and whether it is facing any complaints or disciplinary proceedings. You can verify the lawyer's details with the Law Society, asking for proof of qualifications, academic achievements and association memberships.

Look for lawyers with experience of working with charities.

While all of this is important, the best recommendations are always word of mouth, so ask people at other charities who advises them. Once you have found a couple of promising options, arrange to meet them to check that you can work with them and discuss fees. Remember that the cheapest will not necessarily be the best value. Finally, always take up references.

319. Put contracts in place

Many people believe that contracts are there to stop us falling prey to unscrupulous operators. Consequently, they only insist on contracts with people they don't trust fully. However, this is a misunderstanding of the purpose of contracts. The vast majority of people are honest and trying to do a good job. If you don't trust someone, then don't work with them in the first place – the lack of trust alone will be enough to ensure that the relationship fails.

...contracts are there to prevent conflict between honest and trustworthy people...

In fact, contracts are there to prevent conflict between honest and trustworthy people who simply made different assumptions about a situation, or who emphasised the importance of different aspects of a job. The contract is a written document that should help all parties to understand the relationship and their responsibilities within it.

Whether an agreement is with an employee, a supplier or a beneficiary, put contracts in place, even with those you trust entirely. In fact, especially with those you trust entirely – because they are the last people you want to fall out with.

320. Be alert to employee fraud

Lesley Pickens is the former finance manager of Rathbone, a Manchester-based young people's charity. In February 2009, she admitted 25 counts of fraud and was sentenced to three years in jail. She stole £479,000 over a period of 10 years.

Having joined the charity in 1987, Pickens made 132 transfers from the charity's account into her personal account between March 1998 and April 2008. Her colleagues only became suspicious in June 2007, when a number of transactions could not be accounted for.

...never place your charity's finances at risk by simply believing that no one on your team is committing fraud.

It is tragic, and it should never happen – especially in a charity – but employee fraud does happen. No matter how well you know them, no matter how much you would like to trust them, never place your charity's finances at risk by simply believing that no one on your team is committing fraud. Instead, implement procedures and checks so that you can *know* none of them are.

In fact, it is a common misconception that the smaller the charity, the less susceptible it will be to employee fraud. In reality, smaller charities are likely to have less effective internal processes, which can lead to employees seeing the opportunity and committing fraud.

Most fraud is fairly unsophisticated, though. You can avoid most employee fraud by establishing the following two internal controls and then frequently checking that they are being implemented.

To avoid payroll fraud, where an employee creates a fictitious employee and then arranges for a salary to be paid to that imaginary person, make sure that a senior member of staff signs every employment contract and reviews the payroll every month. You may want to add a second layer of control to protect against that senior member of staff committing the fraud themselves.

To avoid banking fraud, where the employee accesses the charity's account (usually online) and takes money from it, be vigilant when using Internet banking, and make sure that all cheques are signed by two people. In addition, ensure that all bank statements are scrutinised closely for irregular withdrawals.

You can get further guidance from the Charities Commission, from the Community Accountancy Self Help's (CASH) – see: www.cash-online.org.uk, or from your accountant.

321. Prevent workplace injuries

Workplace accidents cost you money. You may have to pay compensation and legal costs. You will spend time dealing with the issue and, of course, the injured employee will be away from work. It is not just major accidents that cost money. Even the smallest accident is an expense that you can do without.

The Health and Safety Executive (HSE) suggests that you take the following five steps to reduce the likelihood of workplace injuries.

Even the smallest accident is an expense that you can do without.

175

1. Find out what could cause harm.
2. Identify who might be harmed – including your employees, visitors or members of the public.
3. Decide what you should do to prevent anything happening to them.
4. Take action in a planned way, recording what you have done.
5. From time to time, check that these actions are still working.

For more advice in this area, download the HSE booklet *Essentials of Health and Safety at Work*, available at www.hse.gov.uk.

For detailed free advice on managing your health and safety obligations towards volunteers, see: www.volunteering.org.uk.

322. Prevent accidents on projects

In early 2009, Tearfund faced court action from a former contractor who was suing the charity for a reported £300,000 in damages. The media consultant had been contracting for Tearfund's partner organisation in Afghanistan, Media for Development. She fell 25 feet down a well in the charity's compound in Kabul when a metal plate covering the well gave way as she stepped on it.

Tearfund admitted that it was negligent in failing to ensure that the well cover was safe and secure, and for not carrying out a proper risk assessment, but denied the claims of injury, loss and damage. Nearly two years after the accident, the claimant said she was still suffering from discomfort and pain in her knee, lower back pain and a nerve pain in her thigh, and had put on 3 stone in weight.

Few charities can afford to pay that much money out...

Few charities can afford to pay that much money out, and while it is impossible to prevent every accident, especially when operating in dangerous parts of the world, every charity has a responsibility to implement appropriate health and safety procedures. Adopt the same procedures with your overseas projects as you do with your places of work in the UK.

... every charity has a responsibility to implement appropriate health and safety procedures.

Chapter 23

Finance

323. Develop accounting skills on your board

One Plus was a charity that famously failed to manage its finances and incurred unnecessary costs. It was one of Scotland's biggest charities, providing services to one-parent families, and in 2005 had a turnover of £11 million. By the end of 2006 it had an overdraft of £2 million, which it was told could not be extended, and in January 2007 the charity went into liquidation with debts of £2.27 million.

A key mistake that One Plus made was to continue to deliver loss-making services. It did this because its management accounts were six months behind schedule, so it had no clear view of its financial position and what it needed to do to stay afloat. With sufficient accounting expertise on its board, the organisation would have understood the perilous situation that it was in and taken steps to rectify the situation.

Do you have anyone with strong accounting skills on your board? If not, take immediate action...

You can learn from the mistakes of One Plus. Look at your board. Do you have anyone with strong accounting skills there? If not, take immediate action – recruit a new board member with these skills immediately, and ask them to make your accounts their focus.

324. Shop around for the best accountant

Of all your advisers, your accountant probably can do more than any other to save you money. You need to make sure you are getting the best advice possible, and you need to be certain that you are getting it at the right price.

Invest some time in reviewing your options. The Institute of Chartered Accountants in England and Wales (www.icaew.com) will be able to provide you with a reference to some good accountants in your area. Consider using one that specialises in doing accounts for charities. Pick a few out, and go through the process detailed in the chapter on procurement.

Look for an accountant who will do more than just the bare essentials. You want one who will look proactively for ways to save you money. You might find that your existing accountant is actually the best option. If that is the case, see what you can do to reduce their fees.

325. Delegate responsibility for budget control

You need to set budgets and monitor spending, but don't try to micro-manage every part of your organisation's spending. For one thing, you are unlikely to have enough time to do it properly, so you will end up rushing decisions, making mistakes and costing your organisation money.

More importantly, if you can delegate responsibility for budget control, you will ensure that you are not the only person in the organisation who wants to save money. If department heads have their own budgets to meet, they too will start focusing on cost savings. Linking their remuneration to the achievement of those budgets may focus their minds even more sharply.

However, you must make sure that everyone with responsibility for controlling a budget has the skills and knowledge that they need to do this. Pick the right people for the job. Give them clear, timely information about what their budget is, what it is for, and how they are expected to report performance to you. If they need any

...must make sure that everyone with responsibility for controlling a budget has the skills and knowledge they need...

training on any aspect of financial management and procurement, don't hesitate to provide it. Investment in these areas will more than pay for itself when you have a team of capable managers all committed to cutting costs in your charity.

326. Know where you stand financially

In autumn 2008, in the space of just a few weeks, the world's economy changed beyond recognition. This had a huge impact on many charities: it affected donation patterns, shifted government funding priorities, and transformed investment priorities.

How well did you respond? Did you receive up-to-the-minute updates on how the economic changes were affecting your financial position, or did you have to wait a few months for your regular quarterly review?

If your answer is the latter, then you almost certainly missed opportunities, and possibly suffered more than you needed to. Your investments may not have performed as well as they could have. You may have been too slow to react to a government funding proposal. A lot has been happening that could have affected your charity; your problem is that you have not been aware of it all.

...every organisation needs clear visibility of its financial position.

In today's fast-moving economy, every organisation (whether a bank, a business or a charity) needs clear visibility of its financial position. Put in place systems to ensure that from now on you always know where you stand financially.

327. Audit your assets

Many organisations are not sure exactly what they own in fixed assets. Of course, you will be aware of what buildings and major pieces of equipment you own – but are you totally certain about the number of laptops, flat-screen monitors, printers, fax machines, mobile phones and so on in your organisation?

Haphazard management of these assets can be more expensive than you imagine, mainly because you may be paying taxes and insurance premiums on items which your charity no longer owns. Organisations very often overestimate their assets by 20 per cent.

Spend a few hours performing an inventory of your assets. Simply list everything that your charity owns. This will be a great deal easier if you have an earlier asset list that you can update, but it still might involve walking round your premises with a clipboard and interviewing each member of staff.

Organisations very often overestimate their assets by 20 per cent.

328. Consider your treasury policy

Mary Reilly, partner and head of charities unit at accountancy firm Deloitte, offers this advice:

> Many charities were badly hit by the financial crisis in Iceland. Every charity has a responsibility to continually monitor their investments and cash holdings to ensure that they are not unduly exposed to risks of this nature. Only the largest charities can be expected to have this sort of expertise in-house, and so for most charities it is usually sensible to take external advice on this.

Every charity has a responsibility to continually monitor their investments and cash holdings...

329. Diversify your investment portfolio

According to figures released by research company Investment Property Databank, returns from charity property funds fell dramatically in 2008. Rensburg Sheppards's Charities Property Fund fell by 17 per cent, CCLA's COIF Charities Property Fund by 23.2 per cent, and Mayfair Capital's Property Income Trust for Charities by a chilling 35.3 per cent.

Clearly, for any charity which had invested in these funds this was extremely bad news. Yet when the investment decision was made – almost certainly at some point before mid-2007 – how could they have known that the property market would nosedive so spectacularly in 2008? They might have guessed, but they have no real way of knowing. The property market had risen year-on-year for 18 years.

Sensible investment always spreads the risk around several markets...

However, at the same time no rational investor would have put all their eggs in one basket. Sensible investment always spreads the risk around several markets, precisely to avoid losses such as these. Protect your organisation from the costs of naive investment decisions, and review your portfolio now to ensure that it is not over-weighted in one market.

330. Make sure your reserves are not too high

...holding excessive levels of reserves puts charities in conflict with their duty to apply income within a reasonable time...

Many charities are highly risk-averse, so they end up holding excessive levels of reserves. Not only does this put them in conflict with their duty to apply income within a reasonable time and to be even-handed to future and current beneficiaries, but it can cost them money.

There have been instances in which donors have become aware that a charity was sitting on large reserves and so they stopped donating. This meant that the charities in question had to spend money reaching new donors.

Furthermore, the perception among the public that charities are wealthy and simply choose not to spend their money makes it more difficult for every charity to raise funds. Keep a close eye on your reserves to ensure they never become too high.

331. Make sure your reserves are not too low

Reserves that are too low can put your survival in jeopardy and deter some donors who might be sceptical about your long-term viability. Setting appropriate reserve levels is a significant ongoing challenge for those running charities.

Put in place an annual review of your reserve levels.

Put in place an annual review of your reserve levels. This should involve comparing your levels to those of similar charities, consulting accounting guidelines, and discussing your position with trustees. Project your future income and expenditure, and try to predict any factors which might substantially raise or lower your reserve levels.

Whatever you do, don't set reserve levels arbitrarily.

332. Communicate your policy on cash reserves

As we have seen in the previous two points, while it is important to ensure your cash reserves are set the right level, it is also important to communicate your policy on this to your stakeholders. Never underestimate the power of the rumour mill. Publish the policy in your annual report, and communicate it through the media and in person to key stakeholders.

Never underestimate the power of the rumour mill.

333. Keep your lines of credit

Even if you currently do not need an overdraft or loan that you have arranged, consider using it. If you don't, the finance provider might start to charge you or withdraw it. Or you might decide that since you don't need it, you may as well close it.

The problem is that when you really need credit you can never get it. That is not just a saying: it is how finance providers work. If they know that someone really needs credit, they see them as high risk and are reluctant to lend to them. At best, they will lend to you at punitively high rates of interest, or will impose very high arrangement fees. At that point you will be wishing that you had simply used your credit lines when you didn't need them.

334. Pay off your highest-interest debt first

... begin paying off the loan with the highest interest.

If you have overdrafts, loans or outstanding credit card balances, it always makes sense to begin paying off the one with the highest interest. That is, the one that is costing you the most, so get rid of it first. Don't allow yourself to be pressurised into paying off cheaper debt earlier – make your decisions based solely on the numbers.

335. Review debt arrangements at least quarterly

... watch out for transfer fees ...

Debt is expensive, so review it at least quarterly to make sure that you are paying as little interest as possible. Simply put aside a time when you can review outstanding balances, and contact alternative providers to see if they will offer you a better deal. However, watch out for transfer fees, and be careful not to get trapped into early repayment penalty clauses.

336. Consider innovative forms of finance

When you need to raise capital for your charity, like most charities and businesses you are likely to go to your bank for an overdraft or loan. If that fails, don't worry that you have reached a dead end. Instead, consider an innovative form of finance known as asset-based lending.

In a nutshell, this involves selling the assets that your organisation owns to a third party and then buying them back over time. It is like remortgaging your home, so it is risky, but that is not deterring more and more organisations from trying it. It is not only the availability of these funds that make them attractive: because the financiers spend time investigating an organisation to understand how it plans to repay the debt, they only tend to make sensible deals, so there is less risk involved.

The sorts of assets against which you can raise finance include equipment, machinery, inventories and property. If you have a trading arm, you may be able to use your invoices. This involves an invoice financier giving you up to 85 per cent of the value of a sales invoice as soon as you raise it. The invoice financier then chases payment and either keeps it all, including the additional 15 per cent, or takes a service charge from it.

Whatever assets you use, make sure that you pick the right finance provider and do the right deal. Be open with your books, and above all else don't overstretch yourself. Get it right, and you may find that these innovative forms of finance are not only a last-ditch option when the bank turns you down, but even a preferable alternative to those overdrafts and loans.

. . . asset-based lending can be a preferable alternative to those overdrafts and loans.

337. Buy the right level of insurance

It is important to have insurance, but do you have too much? Take a close look at all your insurance to check that you have exactly the cover you need. Bear in mind that your needs will change over time, so plan to review your insurance at least once a year. You will need to consider at least the following types of insurance:

. . . your needs will change over time, so review your insurance at least once a year.

- public liability insurance
- employers' liability compulsory insurance
- motor insurance
- travel insurance
- buildings and contents insurance
- equipment insurance
- key person insurance
- business continuity or business interruption insurance
- legal expenses insurance.

Often, an independent insurance broker can help you to get a good deal (see tip 232).

338. Get the best credit card deal

If you use the credit card provided by your bank, you almost certainly are wasting money. Even in the wake of the credit crunch, there are still many 0 per cent deals, cashback schemes and reward programmes out there – so why not take advantage of them? You probably do this for your personal credit card, and you should be equally savvy with your company credit card.

Look for your best deal at: www.compareandsave.com.

339. Review your banking provider

... many charities opt for specialist charity accounts from providers ...

Your choice of current account can have a major effect on the fortunes of your charity. It will determine the level of interest that you earn on positive balances, the amount of time that your staff need to spend doing regular banking, and the ease with which you can borrow money. It is worth considering carefully.

Begin by gaining complete information on the options available. You can look into the main high street banks, but many charities opt for specialist charity accounts from providers such as the Charities Aid Foundation (www.cafonline.org), Triodos Bank (www.triodos.co.uk)

and the Co-operative Bank (www.co-operativebank. co.uk). Find out what they all offer in terms of interest rates, fees, service levels and anything else that matters to you.

340. Know what you want from your bank

The other element to selecting the right bank is knowing what you want from that bank. Is it more important to you to have low fees, or easy access to a bank manager? Are high-credit interest rates more important than low-debit interest rates? Do you need a bank with a local branch, or can you and your colleagues bank online?

Every charity has different requirements, so work out what you need, and avoid making the mistake of believing that all banks are the same. They all have a different approach to their customers, they all offer slightly different products, and what works for one charity might not necessarily be right for you.

Every charity has different requirements, so work out what you need...

341. Talk to your bank manager

It is in no one's interests to see your organisation fail. This does not just apply to your charity's beneficiaries and staff, it also applies to those who lend you money. It is easy to assume that bank managers have better things to do than talk to us, but remember that if you are no longer able to make repayments on your loan or overdraft, they will lose out too.

If find yourself struggling to make repayments, with interest mounting up each month, make an appointment to talk to your bank manager. They should be able to offer some constructive advice on how you can manage the situation more effectively, and they might even be able to suggest alternative products which actually cut your repayments.

...if find yourself struggling to make repayments, talk to your bank manager.

187

Don't leave it until the last minute. The earlier you start talking to your bank manager, the better. Keep them constantly updated on your situation, and you will find them much more willing and able to help if things do become difficult.

342. Don't forget to get paid

...make sure you get paid for services you need to charge for.

'It sounds obvious,' says Gillian Donald, head of charities at accountancy firm Scott-Moncrieff, and chair of the charities committee at the Institute of Chartered Accountants of Scotland, 'but make sure you get paid for services you need to charge for.'

Donald goes on to give the example of One Plus – the Scottish single parents' charity which famously failed to do this and went into liquidation in January 2007 with debts of £2.27 million. She says: 'One Plus had no policy of pursuing people who didn't pay their fees for childcare. It had too many people on the board who cared a great deal about the children it was helping, and too few who understood the commercial imperative of getting the money in.'

She offers the following advice: 'Charities need to think in advance about how they're going to handle these situations. It can be difficult and emotional, because you're dealing with people's lives, so devising a policy in advance makes it much easier to enforce in the heat of the moment.'

343. Don't be afraid to spend to save

In 2007, the ticketing system for the Edinburgh Fringe collapsed on its first day of sales. This caused chaos for ticket buyers, and eventually the Fringe Society was forced to scrap the system. The crisis cost the organisation about £300,000, forced the resignation of its director, Jon

Morgan, and led to a wholesale reorganisation of its management structure.

Gillian Donald at Scott-Moncrieff says:

> The risk assessment of the project was flawed. While the society spent £385,000 on the new system, it was not enough, and so resulted in a system that was not fit for purpose. Had the society spent enough in the first place, they would have saved the £300,000 they lost.

Many charities make this mistake of false economy. We are under continual pressure to spend less, and to direct funds to beneficiaries. However, it is important to conduct proper risk assessments so that you buy what is needed to run your charity most effectively. Don't be afraid to spend to save.

...it's important to conduct proper risk assessments...

344. Stay on top of cashflow

Never relax your focus on cashflow. Poor cashflow is one of main reasons why organisations – both commercial and voluntary – go under. You might have a promise of a grant or a donation, but don't spend it until the funds are cleared in your account.

Every year, prepare a detailed cashflow forecast. This is simply a projection of all the income and expenditure that you expect for the year. If this shows that you will run out of cash at any point, take action.

Every year, prepare a detailed cashflow forecast.

Chapter 24

Tax

345. Stay on the right side of the tax inspector

Tax is undeniably dull, but it is important to get it right. Failure to do so will cost you dearly. Above all else, always account properly for Value Added Tax (VAT), income tax through Pay As You Earn (PAYE) and National Insurance liabilities. These are all statutory liabilities, and errors in accounting may result in large and unexpected liabilities and penalties. For advice, contact HM Revenue & Customs (HMRC). (See: www.hmrc.gov.uk.)

... errors in accounting may result in large and unexpected liabilities and penalties.

346. Take advantage of all tax exemptions

While it is important that you pay enough tax, be very careful not to pay too much. John Conlan, head of charities tax at accountants Baker Tilly says:

Charities spend far more on tax than they need to. They pay business rates, tax on investment income, tax on trading activity, and all sorts of other taxes that they're actually exempt from. The trouble is, they don't know about it.

... be certain you've done everything possible not to overpay tax.

My one piece of advice to everyone running a charity would be to do your research into your tax exemptions, and then get some proper financial advice to be certain you've done everything possible not to over-pay tax. Of course, you should be careful not to end up avoiding taxes for which you are liable, but most charities err in the other direction.

347. Do your accounts yourself

In theory, a good accountant can save your organisation thousands of pounds, but this is not always the case. If you are a fairly small and very straightforward charity, you might find that you can do your annual accounts yourselves and actually save money by not paying an accountant.

There are many courses you can go on to learn the basics, including a number aimed at small to medium-sized charities, run by organisations such as the Directory of Social Change (www.dsc.org.uk) and the Institute of Chartered Secretaries and Administrators (www.ics.org.uk).

...you might find that you can do your annual accounts yourselves...

348. File your accounts on time

The law requires registered charities whose annual income or expenditure exceeds £10,000 to file their accounts and trustees' annual report with the Charity Commission. In addition, charities with an annual income exceeding £10,000 must complete and return an annual return to the Charity Commission.

All documents must be submitted no later than 10 months from the date of their last financial year end. Failure to achieve this can result in a fine, on a sliding scale of up to £7,500. That is an inexcusable waste of donors' money, so make sure you file on time.

349. Keep detailed Gift Aid records

As everyone who works in charities knows – or certainly should, by now – Gift Aid is an excellent source of income. If you are not asking your donors to use Gift Aid then you are already wasting thousands – possibly millions – of pounds.

If you are not asking your donors to use Gift Aid then you are already wasting thousands of pounds.

The way you administer Gift Aid is also vitally important. You must make sure that all your systems are in place for collecting it. HMRC says that you must be able to show an audit trail linking each donation to an identifiable donor who has given a valid Gift Aid declaration, and that all the other conditions for the tax relief are satisfied. If you fail to collect these details, you might be denied Gift Aid. You also might face a fine.

For further details on Gift Aid recordkeeping, go to the charity section of the HMRC website, at: www.hmrc.gov.uk/charities.

350. Use the free Gift Aid CD

Like every charity, you will be keen to encourage all your donors to use Gift Aid. However, communicating this to your donors can be time-consuming and costly. This is why HMRC has produced a CD that explains the importance of Gift Aid and how to use it. Get hold of this free CD by calling the HMRC Charities Helpline on 0845 302 0203, then use it in your fundraising work.

351. Recognise how much you are spending on VAT

... not many charities put sufficient emphasis on reducing their VAT costs.

For most charities, the main tax liability is VAT. However, because standard accounting procedures do not make charities separate out VAT, not many charities are aware of this, and very few put sufficient emphasis on reducing their VAT costs.

John Conlan, head of charities tax at accountants Baker Tilly, says:

> I have one charity client in Birmingham that, if it could see exactly how much it is spending on VAT, would be staggered. It's literally millions of pounds, and it dwarfs all their other tax payments. If more charities realised

how much they pay in this area, my colleagues in the VAT department would be a lot busier!

352. Pay less VAT on fuel and power

David Marrow at the London office of national accountancy firm Beever and Struthers offers this advice:

Fuel and power can be supplied at the reduced 5 per cent rate of VAT if they are supplied for use in charitable non-business activities or for use in a dwelling, such as a care home or hospice. Make sure you are paying VAT on your fuel and power at this rate.

353. Hire VAT advisers on a 'no win, no fee' basis

VAT is extremely complicated. Unless you happen to be a specialist, it is quite possible that you have overpaid your VAT. Hire a VAT adviser to check your payments and see if you are entitled to any rebate. Many of them will do this on a 'no win, no fee' basis, so there is no risk to you.

...hire a VAT adviser to check your payments...

354. Offset finance charges against tax

It is bad enough having to pay interest on overdrafts, loans and bank and credit card charges without paying more tax than you need to as well. You can offset all these finance charges against tax – so make sure you do.

355. Claim your tax allowance for business equipment

Know the rates for which you are allowed to offset purchases of business equipment, such as furniture, IT equipment, tools, machines and so on. The main capital allowance is 20 per cent, but most small companies can

Know the rates for which you are allowed to offset purchases of business equipment...

claim a 40 per cent allowance in the first year of trading, and in some cases, you can claim 100 per cent during the year following purchase. The rates change year by year, so check with your accountant or local tax office – make sure you are claiming as much as you can.

356. Use the Listed Places of Worship grant scheme

In the March 2001 Budget, the Chancellor of the Exchequer introduced a grant scheme that returns in grant aid the difference between 5 per cent and the actual amount spent on VAT on eligible repairs and maintenance to listed places of worship. The scheme is currently due to continue until 31 March 2011.

To find out more and apply see: www.lpwscheme.org.uk.

357. Structure covenants appropriately

There are complicated rules governing what is charitable income and expenditure and what is not. Consider carefully how you structure these, so that the tax situation is most advantageous to you. Essentially, your aim is to pay no tax on anything that is a charitable activity.

To ensure that you achieve this, take advice from a qualified tax adviser. Before approaching one, it is sensible to familiarise yourself first with the rules. You can find a summary of these on the HMRC website at: www.hmrc.gov.uk: type in the search box 'Annex II non-charitable expenditure'.

Essentially, your aim is to pay no tax on anything that is a charitable activity.

Chapter 25

Free advice

358. Get free advice from the Charity Commission

The Charity Commission for England and Wales is established by law as the regulator and registrar of charities in England and Wales. Many charities believe that its role ends there. We can tend to see it as a remote regulator, a little like a charity version of HMRC – best avoided unless you want to end up on the wrong end of a lengthy investigation.

However, there is much more to the Charity Commission than that. Every year, it provides advice and guidance to 24,000 charities. It receives 250,000 calls to its contact centre and 12 million hits on its website, which offers a wide range of advice. It also visits several hundred larger charities. Meanwhile, its programme of regulatory reports highlights good practice, to help charities improve their own performance and learn lessons from others.

Every year, the Charity Commission provides advice and guidance to 24,000 charities.

The Commission publishes information on a wide range of topics that will interest anyone running a charity: for example, its series of publications about preparing charity accounts (type 'SORP 2005' into the search box). It also produces packs which provide a layout and format for the accounts and annual reports of smaller charities producing accruals or receipts and payments accounts. Charities designing their own format for their accounts may find the examples available on the Commission's website helpful.

For pre-printed copies of any of the Charity Commission's publications, call the contact centre on

0845 300 0218, or download them at: www.charity-commission.gov.uk.

359. Get free fleet advice from the Energy Savings Trust

The Energy Savings Trust is a government body that exists to provide organisations such as yours with free advice on how to use less energy. This has a positive effect on the environment, and will help you to cut costs. (See: www.est.org.uk/transport or call the helpline on 0845 602 1425.)

360. Order free materials from the Carbon Trust

The Carbon Trust has produced a series of posters designed to raise awareness of energy efficiency and to encourage employees to adopt simple energy-efficient actions in the workplace. Download them or order printed copies through the website. (See: www.carbontrust.co.uk and type 'posters' into the search box.)

361. Get free advice from the Business Link website

... there's absolutely nothing to stop you benefiting from the free advice on the Business Link website.

Business Link is a government-funded organisation designed to help the UK's small and medium-sized businesses to operate more effectively. It acts as the broker for a wide range of government-funded services, such as the Train to Gain programme, and local branches offer free advice and support.

As a charity, you don't qualify for that free advice and support, but there is absolutely nothing to prevent you from benefiting from the free advice on its website. It covers a vast range of topics that are as applicable to a charity as they are to a business, including:

- finance and grants
- taxes, returns and payroll
- employing people
- health, safety, premises
- environment and efficiency
- IT and e-commerce.

(See: www.businesslink.gov.uk.)

362. Ask your local college what it can do for you

Your local college is packed full of enthusiastic people who are learning new skills and keen for a chance to practise them. It is always worth giving the college a call to ask what it could do for you.

You might find a catering department that would relish the opportunity to provide free catering for your next meeting. You might discover an IT department that would be eager to come in and provide you with a free audit of your hardware and discuss how you could make it more efficient. Or there might be one or two recent leavers who are looking for some work experience, either in your office or one of your projects. Your local college could be a route to low-cost supplies and resources that could go a long way towards cutting your expenditure.

Your local college could be a route to low-cost supplies and resources...

Note that when using a catering college a contract would be needed (even if no payment was being made) in order to prove that the college is a licensed catering establishment with the necessary health and hygiene certificates.

363. Ask your peers for ideas

Consider joining an organisation where you will meet peers...

You might be competing with other charities for donations, but you still will share a strong mutual interest in sharing cost-cutting ideas. Consider joining an organisation where you will meet peers and have the opportunity of sharing best practice and interesting new ideas. You might want to consider:

- the Association of Chief Executives of Voluntary Organisations (www.acevo.org.uk)
- the Institute of Fundraising (www.institute-of-fundraising.org.uk)
- the Charity Law Association (www.charitylawassociation.org.uk)
- the Association of Charity Shops (www.charityshops.org.uk).

Or, if none of those appeal to you, why not set up your own organisation? How many charities are there in your local town or city or in your sector? Why not arrange an informal meeting and see what happens?

364. Copy other charities

Too often, we feel that we have to do all the work ourselves. Or we look at how someone else is doing something and wish we had come up with that idea. Well, stop feeling down about it and simply copy them!

Other charities in your local area will do things very differently from you. Some will have some great cost-saving ideas which have never occurred to you. Find out what they are doing, and copy it.

... imitation is the most sincere form of flattery...

Don't be embarrassed about copying them or think that you are doing something wrong. For one thing, that is how the world works. If makes you feel better, then give them one of your cost-saving ideas in return. For another, imitation is the most sincere form of flattery, so if they do find out that you have pinched their ideas, they are likely to feel complimented.

365. Hold stakeholder meetings to generate cost-cutting ideas

You have read many ideas in this book – 365, to be precise – but there are plenty more out there. Ask for more from your staff and volunteers. Look at what similar charities to yours are doing to cut costs. Also, remember that it can pay to look beyond the world of charity for ideas: your suppliers, your beneficiaries, and even people who just happen to be in your local community, all will have a different point of view from you.

So, set up a forum in which they can share those ideas with you. An online forum would have the benefit of allowing people to add ideas at a time and place of their choosing, but its success would depend on a high level of enthusiasm from potential contributors. You might find it better, initially at least, to get everyone together in a room to brainstorm ideas.

Give them an incentive, such as a few drinks and something to eat, and ask everyone to come up with one idea that is not already in this book. You will be amazed with what they come up with, and the resulting cost savings should more than pay for the cost of the event.

What is more, those ideas will allow you to do even more to save your charity's resources for the purpose they were intended – making the world a better place. As we have seen, cutting costs is never easy. Putting any of these ideas into practice will be hard work, but you have the best incentive possible, and now you have all the ideas you will ever need. Good luck!

...you have the best incentive possible, and now you have all the ideas you will ever need.